James Hogg

The vegetable garden

James Hogg
The vegetable garden
ISBN/EAN: 9783337374808

Printed in Europe, USA, Canada, Australia, Japan

Cover: Foto ©Lupo / pixelio.de

More available books at **www.hansebooks.com**

THE VEGETABLE GARDEN.

A COMPLETE GUIDE

TO THE

CULTIVATION OF VEGETABLES;

CONTAINING

THOROUGH INSTRUCTIONS FOR SOWING, PLANTING, AND CULTIVATING ALL
KINDS OF VEGETABLES; WITH PLAIN DIRECTIONS FOR PREPARING,
MANURING AND TILLING THE SOIL TO SUIT EACH PLANT;
INCLUDING, ALSO, A SUMMARY OF THE WORK TO
BE DONE IN A VEGETABLE GARDEN DURING
EACH MONTH OF THE YEAR.

Entered according to Act of Congress, in the year 1877, by

DICK & FITZGERALD,

in the Office of the Librarian of Congress, at Washington D. C.

PREFACE.

Fifty years' experience and observation in horticultural matters has made us aware that there is a very numerous class of persons throughout the country that need and desire instruction in gardening. These persons are farmers and the business men residing in the neighborhood of our cities, who have plots of ground varying in extent from one-quarter of an acre to two or more acres—people who either do not have land enough to employ, or do not find it convenient to keep a professional gardener, but rely upon the occasional services of a laborer or a groom to cultivate their grounds. These men know but little of garden practice, and hence their employers have to devote their garden plots to the growth of the more common and most easily cultivated vegetables, and this is not often done in the best manner.

It is to such employers that we dedicate this book, so that they may be able to direct and instruct those whom they employ, and provide them with that knowledge and intelligence in which they are lacking.

It were foolishness to attempt to prove that a vegetable garden is a necessity, or that a large variety of vegetables for the table is a luxury and a source of great gustatory pleasure, for that is acknowledged by every one. Yet we have been much struck when visiting or traveling in the country, when noting the very limited supply and the small number of varieties grown by our country friends, especially farmers. Even when there was a good supply, the varieties were of such inferior quality that half the pleasure of the table was done away with. Lettuces that were as tough as a drumhead, tomatoes as empty and tough as an India-rubber ball, gnarly cucumbers, and peas that reminded one of sawdust or dry meal, are not very appetizing adjuncts to a dinner.

This book is not intended for the professional gardener, yet there may be in it some hints or reminders that may be of service to him, for progress is made in gardening as in any other art, and there is much to unlearn as well as to learn. We find ourselves continually being taught some new or improved practice in the art.

We have endeavored to make the book as comprehensive and concise as possible, so that it might be kept within such a limit of cost as would enable the poorest laborer to purchase it—intending it for the million, and not for the professional few.

The times given for sowing and planting are those suitable for the latitude of New York city; due allowance must therefore be made for places north or south of that latitude. As a general rule, a degree southward or northward, as the case may be, is equivalent to five or seven days earlier or later. Climates are sometimes local, being influenced by various circumstances, such as mountains, forests, lakes or the sea; so that the isothermal lines of a country never run exactly on the lines of latitude. In such cases allowances must be made for such local variations.

The seedsmen's catalogues contain the names of a multitude of varieties, many of which are not of much value as compared with others. They have to keep them on hand because there are those who, having cultivated them for many years, are wedded to them, and are slow to acknowledge that improvements can be made; or their particular trade, as in that of market gardeners, requires size or extra earliness, without much reference to their quality. The selections we have given are of such varieties as combine the greatest number of good qualities without reference to size; for this, of itself, in the majority of cases, is but of secondary importance, and very often indicates coarseness and lack of flavor.

We have not given any special directions for forcing or forwarding vegetables in frames, as this requires an amount of skill, labor and attention that few except professional gardeners are possessed of, or are capable of bestowing.

If we find that this book is of service to those for whom it is intended, we shall, at short intervals, issue three other garden handbooks—the "Flower Garden," the "Fruit Garden," and the "Greenhouse and Window Garden."

JAMES HOGG.

New York, March 1st, 1877.

CONTENTS.

	PAGE.
THE VEGETABLE GARDEN...	7
Soils..	7
Situation and Exposure..	9
Laying Out...	10
Implements and Their Use..	11
Preparation of the Soil...	17
Drainage...	18
Manures..	22
Rotation of Crops..	31
Transplanting...	33
Cold Frames and Hot-Beds......................................	35
Seeds and Seed Sowing..	40
Protecting Vegetables..	45
Preservation of Vegetables.....................................	47
Seed Raising..	48
Insects and Insecticides...	50
CULTIVATION OF VEGETABLES.....................................	53
Artichoke...	53
Asparagus..	55
English Broad Beans..	58
Bush Beans..	60
Pole Beans...	61
Beet...	62
Borecole or Kale...	64
Broccoli..	64
Brussels Sprouts...	66
Cabbage..	67
Cardoon..	71
Carrot..	72
Cauliflower..	73
Celery...	75
Celeriac..	80
Chervil...	81
Chiccory...	81
Chives..	82
Colewort...	83
Corn...	83
Cress..	84
Cucumber..	84
Dandelion..	86
Egg Plant..	87

CONTENTS.

	PAGE.
Endive	88
Fetticus	89
Garlic	90
Garden Patience	90
Horse-Radish	91
Jerusalem Artichoke	92
Kohl-Rabi	93
Leek	93
Lettuce	94
Martynia	97
Melons	97
Mushrooms	98
Mustard	100
Nasturtium	100
New Zealand Spinach	101
Okra	101
Onion	102
Orache or French Spinach	105
Parsley	105
Parsnip	107
Peas	108
Peppers or Capsicums	111
Phytolacca	112
Potato	113
Pumpkin	115
Radish	115
Rhubarb	117
Rocambole	119
Ruta-Baga or Swedish Turnip	119
Salsify or Oyster Plant	120
Scolymus	121
Scorzonera	121
Sea-Kale	122
Shallot	123
Sorrel	124
Skirret	124
Spinach	125
Squash	126
Sweet Potato	126
Swiss Chard	127
Tarragon	128
Tomato	128
Turnip	130
Water-Cress	130
Water-Melon	131
Pot Herbs	131
MONTHLY REMINDERS	133

THE VEGETABLE GARDEN.

SOILS.

The success of a kitchen garden largely depends upon the character of the soil and the exposure. Of course in the majority of cases circumstances control the selection, but in a multitude of cases much more suitable selections can be made than are made. Especially is this the case on the part of persons, who, leaving the cities, select suburban or rural residences. Beautiful views, commanding sites, and numerous other considerations too often determine the problem in selecting a rural home, whilst the adaptability of the site for gardening purposes is rarely, if ever, considered; although upon this point much of the enjoyment and comfort of a rural home depends, as well as the cost of keeping it up.

Sandy soils, especially those having a loose, gravelly subsoil, are the least retentive of moisture, and accordingly seriously suffer from drought: but there are cases in which sites having a deep sandy soil, and surrounded by higher land, are constantly moist, as the water from the higher lands drains or percolates through the substratum of the sand, and the action of the sun, in causing evaporation from the surface, draws up the moisture from below, bringing it in contact with the roots of the crops, thereby keeping them constantly moist, and preventing them from suffering in a dry time, and so producing excellent crops of vegetables. Sandy soils are well adapted for raising early vegetables, but are not suited for many midsummer crops.

The more clayey a soil is, the longer it will retain water and the longer it will be in becoming fit to work in the spring; hence such soils are not adapted for raising early crops, but will produce late crops, such as celery and late cabbage. There is, however, a great difference even in heavy clay soils. In some the texture or grain is coarse, and in others it is very fine. The finer the particles of which the clay is composed, the more tenacious of water it will be, and the longer in drying or fitness for working, and when dry it will be liable to bake or harden under the sun's heat, and so involve great labor in cultivating it.

The most suitable soil for gardening purposes is a deep, sandy loam, with a somewhat gravelly subsoil. Such a soil is generally equably moist, will hold moisture longer without becoming hard when dry, and speedily gets into working order.

Air, heat and moisture at the roots, as well as at the tops, are all necessary to plant-growth; hence, the easier a soil can be pulverized to a considerable depth, the better it is adapted for cultivation. This is of such great importance, that when a choice can be had, always select for a garden site one with a good friable subsoil, such as a sandy or gravelly clay, through which the surface water will freely percolate. In such cases even a poor surface soil can be made to produce good crops, and a large expenditure of money can be saved in the item of drainage. Always avoid spongy or water-lodged land, especially if it is clayey, as such land requires a large expenditure of money in drainage operations, and even then is generally cold and unfitted for early crops.

Thus poor soils of any kind, unless with a good subsoil, cannot be made to bear a large variety of crops, no matter what amount of manure is applied. They should be devoted to fibrous-rooted crops, such as lettuce, spinach, onions, peas, etc.; for tap-rooted crops, like beets, parsnips and carrots, will not succeed in them.

A light or sandy soil will be benefited if worked when moist, as it makes it more compact; on the contrary a clay soil should be worked when dry, otherwise it becomes pasty, and if hot, dry weather ensues, it hardens or bakes, thus preventing the germination of seeds, and checks the growth of plants by becoming almost impervious to the action of the air, heat and moisture.

SITUATION AND EXPOSURE.

The kitchen garden should always be sheltered from northerly or westerly winds. Naturally, if possible, by woods or belts of evergreens, and when these cannot be had, then by close fences on the northern and westerly boundaries, to such an extent, at least, as to furnish shelter for frames and borders for raising a sufficiency of early vegetables, according to the size or demands of the family. When sheltered by woods or belts of trees, deep trenches should be dug between the trees and the garden, to prevent the roots of the former from penetrating into the soil of the latter, for it is astonishing to what a great distance they will send their roots to obtain the benefits of the manure applied to the garden, and so rob the crops of their proper sustenance.

The best exposure is one sloping to the south or southeast; next, one to the south-west. The exposures to the northerly points of the compass are proportionally bad as they approach the north point, which is almost useless for general gardening purposes.

The kitchen garden should be as near the dwelling as possible, when not inconsistent with the laying out of the grounds, should they be of any extent; and even then provision can often be made for its proximity to the house by masking it with ordinary trees and shrubs. Proximity to the house is desirable for convenience' sake, for preventing depredations, and for affording an oversight of the workmen, when a regular gardener is not kept. It is also well to have it as near to the stables as possible, provided poultry are not kept there, unless in enclosed runs, as they are a great annoyance and source of damage to a garden. Where they can be had, a pond, a stream of water, or a well are desirable accessories to a kitchen garden, as they frequently save a large amount of labor in carrying water from a distance.

LAYING OUT.

The simplest and best form for a kitchen garden, is a parallelogram, with a wide walk through the centre. In large gardens this should be seven or eight feet wide, to admit the passage of a cart or wagon. In smaller gardens it should be at least five feet wide, in order to allow of the free passage of a wheelbarrow. Right and left from this centre walk the beds for the different sorts of vegetables may be laid out. A border from four to six feet wide should be laid out next to the boundaries, for the growing of the smaller vegetables—borders facing to the south or south-east being very desirable for growing early vegetables, and those with a northerly aspect for such plants as require shade. Between these side borders and the main borders there should be a walk three or four feet wide, for the sake of convenience.

Where there is an abundance of land, it is better to enlarge the size of the garden in order to work it with the plow, to do which is much less expensive than to cultivate it with the spade, and it can be far more rapidly done; an object of great importance to our farming community, whose agricultural operations overdrive them in the spring-time, and so unfortunately allow them but little time to devote to horticultural work.

On no account should currant, gooseberry, raspberry or other bushes, or any fruit trees, be planted in the kitchen garden, for they are a continual annoyance and nuisance, always in the way, always robbing the adjoining vegetables of their proper nutriment, shading them, and being themselves continually injured by the spading and other garden operations necessary to growing vegetables. Always provide a fruit garden for them, and grow them in separate quarters, where each sort can receive its own special cultivation.

IMPLEMENTS AND HOW TO USE THEM.

All garden tools should be made of the best materials, and be as light as possible, consistent with strength. There is no economy in using a spade weighing twelve pounds, when one weighing eight pounds will do the work, and be equally strong. If in spading a piece of ground we turn over two thousand spadesful of earth, and in doing so use a wrought iron, steel-edged spade, weighing one pound more than a cast steel one, we have simply wasted our strength in lifting one ton of iron which has not been of the least use to us, and so with every other tool. If we take into consideration the numerous strokes which a man hoeing has to take during a day's work, a difference of one or two ounces in the weight of a hoe becomes quite an item in the useless expenditure of strength. Spades, forks, hoes and rakes should, therefore, always be made of the best cast steel.

Spades for digging purposes, in pulverizing the soil, are now but seldom used among the better class of gardeners, the spading fork being substituted for it. This fork is about the size and shape of a spade, having four or five flat tines, about three-quarters of an inch wide. Being so much lighter than a spade, and exposing so much less surface to the friction incident to pushing it into the soil, it saves a large amount of muscular expenditure, and our own experience is that a man will do one-third more digging in a day with one of these forks than with the lightest made spade, and do it with far less fatigue. The work is also better done than with the spade, especially if the soil is in any way wet, for the spade turns it over in heavy, cheesy lumps, whereas the fork, in lifting it, breaks it up and pulverizes it more readily.

This kind of fork cannot be readily used as a manure fork, on account of the width of the tines, and neither can a manure fork be used for spading purposes, on account of its curvature and the narrowness of the tines—hence it is necessary to provide a manure fork for the handling of the manure used.

The operation of digging is apparently a very simple one, yet very few of our laboring men really understand it. They will take the spade and run it into the ground in such a way as to take up a slice two or three inches thick, turn it over, break it down and level it, and so leave the soil underneath quite untouched, hard and nearly impenetrable to the roots of the crop sown or planted on the surface. The spade or fork should be entered into the ground in nearly a perpendicular direction to its full depth, taking a breadth or spit of soil not more than four inches thick, and then lifting and turning it over, breaking and leveling it down—or, in other words, pulverizing it to as great a depth and as finely as possible.

Of hoes there are many patterns, used for different purposes; the well-known corn hoe is useful for earthing up plants and similar purposes, but they are usually too large and clumsy for general garden use. For weeding purposes we prefer a six inch English draw hoe, about four inches wide. These are made of saw-blade steel, riveted to a wrought iron back, having an eye into which the handle is set. They are very light and can easily 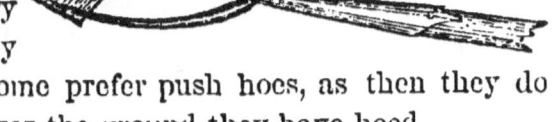 be kept sharp. Some prefer push hoes, as then they do not have to walk over the ground they have hoed.

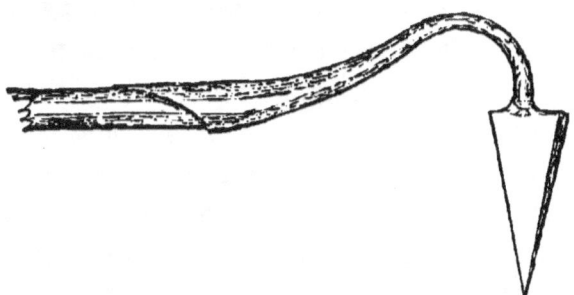

For stirring the soil the bayonet hoe is very useful, especially for seed beds and among very young plants. To use between the rows of the regular crops the prong hoe is an excellent implement; it is also useful in turning over manure, digging potatoes, and for a variety of purposes. Another useful tool for weeding in seed-beds, or to assist in hand weeding, is a weeding hook of the following pattern, known as the Excelsior Weeding Hook.

Iron rakes have almost gone out of use in this country, having been largely superseded by cast steel rakes, which are much lighter and do better work. Two or three sizes are necessary in a garden of any size, to enable the operation of raking to be done in the various widths of rows at which the crops are planted. One each of six, ten and fourteen teeth will be convenient sizes.

To rake off weeds and rubbish no directions are necessary, but to rake a bed or border level requires some skill or sleight of hand. To pulverize the surface soil the rake should be firmly held in the hands, the teeth of the rake deeply pressed into the soil, and worked backward and forward until the desired pulverization is produced, this depending upon the size and character of the seed to be sown. In dressing off a bed, the rake should be lightly and more uprightly held in the hands, and the teeth but slightly pressed into the soil, and any small stones or hard clods of earth drawn off by a sudden jerk of the rake; both cases requiring practice and care to avoid getting the surface into cat-hills.

A wooden roller is a very useful implement in a garden.

It can be readily and cheaply made in the following manner: Take a round log of hard wood eight to ten inches in diameter and four or five feet long, and insert in the centre of each end a gudgeon projecting a couple of inches, to take the eyes of an iron frame and cross handle by which to pull it.

A marker for marking out seven rows at once is made by taking a piece of wood about three inches square and six feet long, and boring holes in it on one side, a foot apart, and inserting in them hard wood teeth—like harrow teeth—six inches long; and on the other side inserting them nine inches apart. It should have two handles, so as to enable it to be drawn straight. The teeth thus

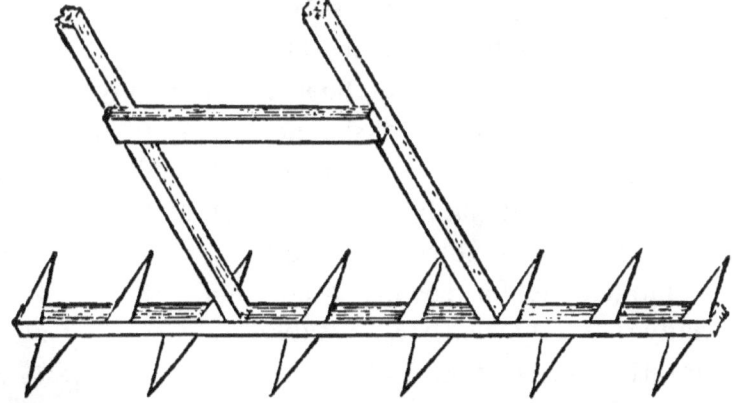

set will answer for nearly all row spaces. If nine inch or twelve inch row spaces are wanted, it marks them out as it is made; if eighteen inch or twenty-four inch spaces are needed, we have only to skip every other line marked. In using it, stretch a garden line tightly the length wanted, and set the outer tooth against it and draw the marker steadily and firmly to the end; on returning, set the end tooth in the outer row as a guide, and so on until the desired number of rows are marked off.

A dibber, for transplanting small plants, is readily made

by taking a piece of crooked hard wood about ten or twelve inches in length, and sharpening it to a blunt point. In using it, after pushing it into the ground perpendicularly to make the hole for the plant, the plant should be held in the hole and the dibber again inserted about two inches from the plant in an angular direction and then drawn in at the top towards the plant; this presses the soil against the roots and insures it being firmly set in the soil, for if not so set it will be likely to wilt and die. It is possible, and is often done by careless garden laborers, to press the soil against the collar of the plant and leave the roots hanging in an open space below, and if such careless men press the soil down with their feet, they do it so heavily as to compress the soil, if it is any way wet, to the consistency of an unbaked brick. In either case, as we have often experienced to our loss, both the plants and the labor are thrown away.

The Sidney Seed Sower is a very useful implement for sowing seeds, especially in windy weather, as it distributes the seeds of any size from peas to cabbage seed with great regularity, either broadcast or in drills.

To these may be added a wheelbarrow, a water pot, a garden reel and line, a garden trowel, and an eight or ten inch coarse, flat file. We find the latter an essential tool to sharpen hoes and spades, for if they are not kept well sharpened they require a much larger amount of labor in using them. An oil cask is also useful for mixing liquid manures in.

Where the garden can be made large enough to be worked by the plow, the ordinary farm implements, such as a small plow, a cultivator and a harrow, are all that are necessary. They need no description or instructions as to their use, any farm laborer being able to use them.

PREPARATION OF THE SOIL FOR A GARDEN.

If the site selected for the garden is a piece of grass land, it should, some time between the first of September and the end of November, be plowed, and if manure can be had, it should be spread on the land previous to commencing to plow. The plowing should be shallow, cutting the sod in thin slices and turning it over flat, and then harrowing it either with the back of the harrow or with one having very blunt teeth, so as to fill up the hollows between the furrows, and to reduce it to as level a state as possible without pulling the sod out of its overturned position. Early in the spring it should be crossed-plowed and subsoiled, by either using a subsoil plow or running an ordinary plow through the open furrow made by the first plow. This renders the soil friable to a greater depth than it otherwise would be. But care must be had not to bring the subsoil to the surface, as it is always inferior to the surface soil, and generally takes a great length of time, and a large amount of cultivation and manuring, to make it fertile. All that is required is to break it up and get it into such a state as that tap-rooted plants can easily penetrate it.

If, instead of this second plowing, it is worked by hand, then a trench eighteen inches wide and one spade deep should be taken out and laid to one side; the subsoil should then be spaded with a spading fork. A layer of manure may then be laid upon this broken-up subsoil, and the top soil from the adjoining eighteen inches in width thrown over it; the subsoil under it then broken up and manured, the top soil from the third eighteen inches thrown upon it, and so on *seriatim*, trench after trench, until the plot is finished, returning the top soil taken from the first trench to the last one. This may appear to involve a large amount of labor and a great deal of expense, but it will be found to well repay both in the excellent crops produced.

After the land has been thus prepared, either by plowing or by hand labor, it should be planted with potatoes, corn or late cabbages the first season, as it can scarcely be brought into sufficiently fine tilth for ordinary vegetables the first year.

If the subsoil should be heavy and retain water, it will be necessary to under-drain it, the modes of doing which we will now explain.

DRAINAGE.

Drainage is necessary whenever the subsoil is of such a character as to hold water. It is not only low-laying land that requires it, for often land laying on the lower declivity of a hill-side will need it, because the water draining from the upper part of the hill, will, when the subsoil does not admit of its passing off freely, ooze out on the surface soil below, and make it cold and wet. This coldness of the soil is produced by the evaporation of the water through the action of the sun's rays or the action of the wind. This has been the subject of numerous experiments, the results of which have shown that the evaporation of one pound of water contained in one hundred pounds of earth, already containing its proper quantity of moisture, lowered its temperature ten degrees, and that the difference in temperature of the same land, drained and undrained, varied from six to ten degrees, equivalent to an elevation of from 1900 to 2500 feet. A rainfall of two inches on an acre of land would weigh two hundred tons, and require over twenty tons of coal to evaporate it; at least one-third of this amount of heat would be abstracted from the soil, the balance being furnished from the atmosphere. In a wet time an acre of some soils will contain one thousand spare hogsheads of water, which the sooner it is got rid of the better for the soil and the crops growing in it. Such an amount of surplus water in the soil, if taken from it by evaporation alone, would take over a month, as the rate of evaporation per acre on a midsummer's day is about twenty-five hogsheads. So that the necessity of artificial under-drainage is very apparent on soils where the substratum does not afford a natural outlet.

The advantages of under-draining are that it makes the soil warmer by decreasing the evaporation, and so makes it earlier; it prevents injuries from drought because a larger amount of moisture is contained in the soil, owing to the greater depth to which it is absorbed; it causes the manure in the soil to decompose more rapidly, for manure decomposes very slowly when saturated with water, and the water draining through the soil takes down with it the various gases it has absorbed from the atmosphere, all of which are elements of plant food.

It often requires much study and consideration to lay out a plan of drainage, as this has to be decided according to circumstances, which are seldom exactly alike in any two localities; the relative position of the site in regard to higher and lower levels of the land adjoining, the undulations of the land composing the site, the means of getting rid of the drainage water, and the character of the subsoil all being elements which must enter into the calculation.

When the site is on the side or foot of a hill, it is generally necessary to cut off the water that drains from the higher level, by constructing drains across the hill and connecting these with drains at right angles running down through the garden site. The accompanying diagram more fully explains this.

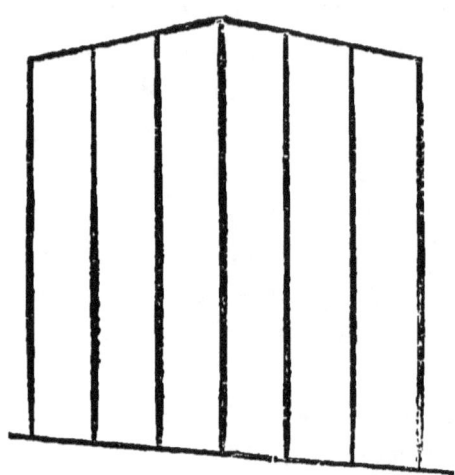

The two upper sloping lines represent two drains on the higher level which intercept the water draining from the hill, and the parallel lines running down the descent through the garden, indicate drains either discharging into a pond or brook, or connecting with a main drain which conveys the water to some proper outlet of discharge. If the land is on a ridge the lateral drains should be right up

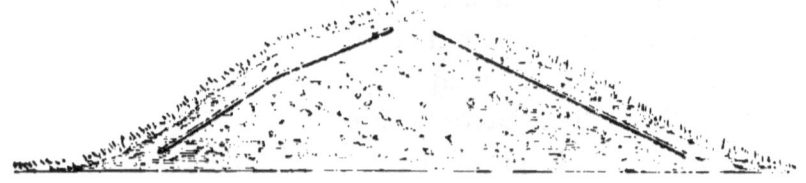

and down the slope of the land, and connect with main drains in the depression, as in the above diagram.

Open ditch drains are not to be recommended, as they only conduct the water away, and scarcely, if at all, produce the effect of under-drainage, and, besides, are in the way of plowing or similar operations, readily fill up, and their sides become a regular garden of weeds. Where small stones are plenty, trenches dug out to the requisite depth, and filled in a foot deep with stones, overlaid with sod, the turf side down, will answer a useful purpose. But no sort of drain is equal to, and in the end is so economical as 1¼ inch round draining tiles, with collars for the laterals, connecting with 2½ inch tiles for the mains. These tiles are laid

jointed together, the water percolating through the joints and passing off through the tiles. The proper depth to lay them is three feet, if the drains are twenty feet apart, and four feet deep, if the drains are forty feet apart, with a fall of six inches to the hundred feet, although less will do; but then they will require very great care in the laying of them. The drains should run parallel with each other if possible, and down the deepest descent of the land. In laying them, care must be had to have the bottom of the trench as truly level and firm as possible, in order to prevent sagging or undulations, as, if laid unevenly, the silt will settle in the lower portions and choke the drain.

It is not so much the distance apart of the drains, as their depth, which affects their efficiency—hence, drainings laid four feet deep and forty feet apart will be as efficacious as those laid three feet deep and twenty feet apart. The character of the subsoil must determine this. In heavy, stiff soils, they should be placed twenty feet apart and three feet deep, as the trenches will cost less to excavate, and the hard subsoil might prevent the free passage of the water into the drains.

MANURES.

It is useless to expect success in gardening, unless there is a plentiful supply of manure liberally applied to the soil. It is this which induces a rapid growth and produces that succulence and crispness so desirable in vegetables. In a large majority of cases it is difficult to obtain, unless in the neighborhood of towns and cities, and especially on farms, for farmers generally need all they get from their stables for their farm crops, and begrudge what is necessary for the garden. Hence it is of great importance to husband every substance that has fertilizing powers, and so prepare it that it will produce its greatest effects.

Of all materials containing fertilizing powers, none is equal to the excrements of animals, for they contain all the elements of plant life, but not always in the proper proportions, therefore they need to be combined and prepared for the special uses to which they are to be applied. In the preparation of them it is necessary to bring them into a less concentrated and more comminuted form than they are naturally, and at the same time preserve the gases they contain; these gases being the principal elements in plant food.

Comminution of the mass is brought about by fermentation, and this is only another term for combustion or burning. This we see in horse manure that has been piled up and allowed to become overheated; on opening such a pile of manure, we see in it white masses or streaks which are only the ashes of the manure, the rest of the material having been volatilized or dissipated into the atmosphere in the form of various gases, these composing the major part of the plant food in it. It is the same process that takes place in the combustion of coal or wood, only in a less and slower degree, the product, heat, being the same.

The gases, either by themselves or in combination, are fetid, and are evolved as soon as the excrements are voided. When, therefore, manure gives out offensive odors, we may be sure that its gaseous parts are escaping, and that it is losing its fertilizing powers. To prevent this, or to recover them as they are given off, is to economize and add to our stock of fertilizing materials. A similar loss ensues from the evaporation of the liquid parts of the manure, for the water it contains in evaporating carries with it large quantities of these gases, which it absorbs as they are evolved, and retains even when it is in the form of vapor. Leaching also produces the same effect—hence the benefits arising from the use of liquid manure.

Manures should therefore not be exposed to the action of the weather, for then they lose from one-half to two-thirds of their strength. They should be kept dry, and mixed with such materials as will absorb the gases thrown off in the process of fermentation. To this end it is true economy to provide a good-sized open shed, in which the manure should be kept and prepared for use.

The best absorbents of the gases arising from the decomposition of the manure, are dry earth, peat, muck, charcoal dust, leaf mould, spent bark and sawdust. Of these dry earth is always to be obtained in summer time, when it can be laid away under cover for winter use. Peat and muck are generally to be had on farms of any extent. They should never be used when fresh dug, but should be thrown up in ridges to be exposed to the action of the air and frost to pulverize them. They should then be composted with a mixture made of lime and salt, as directed in the next paragraph, using four bushels of the mixture to one cord of the peat or muck; this should be done under cover, so as to keep off rain, which would cause the mixture to leach out and so weaken its strength. It should be allowed to lay for a month or six weeks, when it may be used in mixing with the manure, the quantity to be used depending upon the character and quality of the manure; enough must be used to prevent the escape of any offensive odors, which, as we have already stated, indicates the escape of the fertilizing gases; but as a general rule, one-third of green or fresh manure to two-thirds of the peat or muck will be a proper proportion.

To make the dissolving mixture referred to above, take three bushels of lime, as freshly burned as possible, and slake it with water in which one bushel of salt has been dissolved, using only just enough of water to dissolve the salt. Mix it well and keep it under cover, and let it be ten or fifteen days old before using. Lime alone will decompose peat or muck, but it is far less powerful than when combined with salt as above. It should *always* be applied in a dry and fresh state, not air or water slaked.

Unleached wood ashes, applied at the rate of twenty-five bushels to a cord of muck, will also decompose it. The sparlings or refuse of potash warehouses, applied at the rate of from twenty to one hundred pounds to a cord, will also have a like effect.

When dry earth is used as an absorbent, it should be mixed about half and half with the manure, moistening it with a weak solution of sulphuric acid—oil of vitriol—about one pound of acid to forty-five or fifty gallons of water. This takes up the volatile ammonia which arises from the manure, and converts it into sulphate of ammonia, which is soluble but not volatile, yet is one of the most powerful fertilizers. Or gypsum—plaster of Paris—as prepared for agricultural purposes, may be added to the dry earth to increase its absorbing powers, and to fix the ammoniacal vapors. A hundred pounds to a cord of dry earth will be sufficient.

Where horses, cows and pigs are kept, it is not necessary to keep their manure separate, but it is best to throw it into one common pile and treat it as we have suggested. The urine of the animals is of very great value, and every care should be taken to save it, by using saw-dust, dry earth or other absorbents in the stalls. All the soap-suds, chamber-lye and kitchen slops should be thrown on the compost heap, as they largely aid in making up its effectiveness. Poultry manure is sometimes needed for special crops, it should therefore be kept by itself, mixing it liberally with dry earth or gypsum, or these may be used with great advantage by frequently sprinkling them on the floor of the poultry house.

Night soil is the most powerful of all manures, and arrangements should always be made to preserve it by the use of dry absorbents, such as dry earth, dry muck or charcoal dust. A liberal use of these will destroy its offensiveness, and enable it to be used as readily as any other manure. The earth-closets, now coming so generally into use, soon save their cost in rendering this manure available. When used, it should be very largely diluted with an absorbent, as otherwise it will kill the plants to which it is applied.

Lime acts chiefly as a decomposing agent, as it dissolves the silica and other constituents of the soil and the vegetable matter in it, and so renders them fit for plant food.

Shell lime is the purest and best, but all limes should be used freshly burnt, as when air-slaked they are almost inert. When used alone it should always be applied as a top dressing, and should never be mixed alone with other manures containing ammonia, as it liberates the ammonia, for which reason it should always be accompanied with absorbents when composted with manure.

Soot is an excellent manure for many vegetables, such as cabbages, melons, onions, etc., as it contains sulphur and also destroys insects.

Salt is useful as a manure for some vegetables, such as asparagus and sea-kale. It is best applied mixed with the compost used in manuring them, at the rate of a bushel of salt to a cord of compost; if more than this quantity is used, it will be apt to pickle the manure and so prevent its decomposition.

Bones are a most excellent manure, but must be dissolved or be finely ground before being used. Where few bones accrue, as in an ordinary family, and unleached ashes can be had, bones can be dissolved in the following way: Take a large cask, set it in a cool, shady place, and in it place a layer of bones, four or five inches deep, and on these place a layer of the same depth of the unleached ashes, wetting them with as much water as they will take up without leaching through, and so continue a layer of bones and a layer of ashes alternately. In ten or twelve months they will be dissolved, except, perhaps, a few near the top, which may form the bottom layer for the next year. The bones and ashes should be shoveled out, some more dry ashes added and well mixed together, and the compost is ready to use. A more rapid mode of dissolving them, is to place them in a tub, and moisten them with a solution of one-third their weight of sulphuric acid in five or six times its weight of water. The acid thus diluted should only be sprinkled on them a little at a time, until the bones become a soft, pasty mass, which can be mixed with dry peat or earth, and then used as a manure.

Bone-dust or finely ground bone is sold commercially by persons who have mills made purposely for the purpose of crushing and grinding them. The crushed bones are generally about half an inch long, mixed with the powder or dust of the bones resulting from crushing them. The bone-dust or meal is the bones reduced to a powder resembling Indian meal. This latter is best adapted for gardening purposes, as it produces more immediate effects upon the crops. Crushed bones and bone-dust will ferment if thrown into a heap and moistened; hence, in order to the more evenly distribute them on the land, and to make them produce a more immediate or quicker effect, they may be composted with moist earth for two or three weeks before using. When used for cabbage, cauliflowers, turnips and plants of the same family, some cultivators add sulphur to the bone-dust in the proportion of seven pounds of flour of sulphur to one hundred pounds of bone-dust, previous to fermenting it. The mass will give off strong fumes of sulphur, and when applied to the soil keeps off the attacks of the turnip-fly. We also think that the sulphur acts as a special manure to plants of the kind indicated, as they all contain sulphur in their composition, as is evidenced in the sulphureted-hydrogen gas which they throw off when in a state of decay, or in their effect of tarnishing silver when brought in contact with them.

Horn shavings are similar in their character and action to bones; they should be mixed with five or six times their bulk of earth, and allowed to ferment five or six weeks before using. They make a most excellent manure for potatoes and corn. Tanner's waste should be treated in the same way. Or either may be rotted by composting them with manure, in the proportion of one part of shavings or waste to fifteen parts of manure.

Super-phosphate is a commercial manure, made by adding sulphuric acid to burnt bones as used in the sugar refineries, although it can be made from fresh bones. It is somewhat uncertain in its effects in some soils, as it will sometimes be inert the first season after being applied, and only act the second year. Some manufacturers mix with it the blood and animal waste of the slaughter-houses. This ensures its immediate action and adds greatly to its value.

Fish-guano is the dried refuse of the fish-oil manufacturers, finely ground. It is a powerful fertilizer, and is also best used when composted with earth.

Guano is well known as a powerful fertilizer. Its great value consists in the amount of ammonia it contains. It should always be used composted with earth, to which gypsum or a weak solution of sulphuric acid has been added, in order to change the ammonia from a volatile state to a fixed and soluble one. It is immediate in its effects. Never use ashes or any alkali with guano.

Poudrette is the desiccated night soil from the cities. In preparing it charred peat is generally used as an absorbent. It is an excellent manure, producing immediate effects, and does not need composting. Unfortunately it is not always of certain value, as the night soil from the cities is often mixed with sand, coal ashes and similar refuse.

Hops, as the refuse of the breweries, when they can be obtained, are a very powerful manure, by some considered to be even more valuable than horse manure. They should be rotted down very slowly, for if allowed to ferment strongly they lose a large portion of their value. It is best, perhaps, to compost them with stable manure.

Street sweepings are very uncertain in their strength, and we place but little value upon them as a fertilizer, the manure being in very uncertain proportions to the sand and earth swept up with it. It besides has generally its strength dried out or washed out before being swept up. When dried it makes a good absorbent for the compost heap.

Gypsum, or plaster, is not of much value to garden crops, except as an ingredient in the compost heap, where its facility of absorbing ammonia renders it of great value.

Sulphur has lately been recommended as a manure for all plants of the cabbage family, for which we have no doubt it may prove of value. It has been applied in the form of flour of sulphur, at the rate of six to eight pounds per acre. Sulphuric acid is sometimes used on limestone soils at the rate of thirty to forty pounds, diluted with two hundred times its weight of water, or two gallons to three or four hundred gallons of water.

Spent tan-bark and sawdust will make good manure, when treated with the lime and salt mixture already described. It neutralizes any injurious acids that may be in them. But it is better to use such materials as these, sea-weed and similar matters, as bedding for the animals, as they largely absorb the urine from them.

In applying manure to the soil, never apply more than may be judged sufficient for the present crop, as it is poor economy to bury your capital in the soil. This is especially the case in light sandy soils. Manures should also be alternated—that is to say, the same sort of manure should not be continuously applied to the same piece of land, but some other kind occasionally used, in order to furnish the soil with all the elements of plant growth.

Liquid manures are also of service to many crops, but should always be used freely diluted.

All manures for garden purposes should be immediately plowed or spaded in after they are applied.

The quantities of each kind to be applied to an acre are given below. They vary much in their range, as the present condition of the soil as to fertility must be taken into consideration, and this must be left to the judgment of the cultivator.

Barn-yard manure; five to twenty tons, or thirty to forty cubic yards.

Bone-dust; sixteen to twenty bushels, or seven hundred to twelve hundred pounds.

Fresh fish; twenty-five to forty bushels.

Fish guano; four to six hundred pounds.

Guano; three to eight hundred pounds.

Gypsum; five to six hundred pounds.

Horn shavings; twenty-five to forty bushels.

Hops; thirty to forty tons.

Lime; fifty to one hundred and fifty bushels.

Night-soil; twenty bushels.

Poudrette; twenty-five to thirty-five bushels.

Salt; two to six bushels.

Soot; twenty to fifty bushels.

Sulphur; six to eight pounds.

Sulphuric acid; thirty to forty pounds.

Super-phosphate; five hundred to a thousand pounds.

Tanner's refuse; five to eight hundred pounds.

Wood ashes; twenty to forty bushels.

We have devoted a large space to this subject, but its importance requires it. If there is anything in which amateur cultivators are lacking, it is in having a liberal supply of manure, the very corner-stone of all gardening operations. It is therefore of the first importance to know how to make the most of it.

ROTATION OF CROPS.

The necessity of the rotation of crops was long ago recognized, and was supposed to arise from the plants giving out excrementitious matters from their roots into the soil, and so poisoning it. But it is now found that plants give out but little of such matters, and that the necessity of rotation principally arises from the plants of any particular class exhausting the soil of those substances which are necessary for their own particular nourishment, no two classes of plants requiring the same combination of substances for their particular support. Mr. Bridgeman, in his "Young Gardener's Assistant," has so tersely given instructions on this point, that we here subjoin them.

Fall spinach is an excellent preparative crop for beets, carrots, radishes, salsify, and all other tap as well as tuberous-rooted vegetables.

Celery or potatoes constitute a suitable preparation for cabbage, cauliflower, and all other plants of the Brassica family; as also for artichokes, asparagus, lettuce and onions, provided the ground be well situated for them.

Lands that have long lain in pasture are, for the first three or four years after being tilled, superior for cabbage, turnips and potatoes, and afterward for culinary vegetables generally.

Fibrous-rooted plants should be alternated with tap or tuberous-rooted ones, and *vice versa*.

Plants which produce luxuriant tops, so as to shade the

ground, should be succeeded by such as yield small tops, or narrow leaves.

Plants which during their growth require the operation of stirring the earth should precede such as do not admit of such culture.

Ground which has been occupied by artichokes, asparagus, rhubarb, sea-kale, or such other crops as remain long on a given spot, should be subjected to a regular rotation of crops, for as long a time at least as it remained under such permanent crops. These should be renewed on the same principle as often as they fail to produce luxuriantly. No two crops should be allowed to ripen their seeds in succession, in the same soil.

Manure should be applied to the most profitable and exhausting crops. Root and seed crops are always more exhausting than leaf crops.

The following ten years' rotation is from an English work, and we give it to our readers as an example of how a piece of ground should be managed:

1—peas and beans; 2—broccoli, cabbage and winter greens; 3—carrots, parsnips, beets, scorzonera, salsify, skirret, parsley; 4—onions, cauliflower, turnips; 5—spinach, spring onions, and other secondary crops; 6—savoy, broccoli, winter greens, red cabbage, leeks; 7—potatoes; 8—turnips, cabbage, broccoli; 9—celery, cardoons; 10—French beans, etc., as at first.

The secondary crops mentioned above are those of short duration, such as lettuces, radishes, salads, annual herbs, etc. These can be frequently planted between the rows of the main crops, and taken off before they interfere with each other.

TRANSPLANTING.

This is an operation requiring much care and attention, for if these are not given, success is very doubtful. Many vegetables are the better for being transplanted from a seed-bed, instead of being sown where they are to remain. Of this class are all the Brassica or cabbage family, lettuce, endive, celery, cardoons, tomatoes, onions and leeks. Peas and beans are improved in precocity by it. Ruta-bagas, radishes, parsnips, beet, scorzonera, salsify and skirret can be transplanted, and so vacancies in the rows can be filled up, but the operation does not effect any particular improvement. Turnips, carrots, spinach, cress and mustard cannot be transplanted with any success.

In transplanting, the first requisite is to see that the plants are properly dug up, in such a way as to secure all the roots. We do not approve of shortening the roots in the process, and think that, unless in very exceptionable cases, the tops should not be shortened either. If the soil of the seed-bed, at the time of transplanting, is not quite moist, it should receive a good soaking of water two or three hours before the plants are to be taken up. These should be carefully lifted with a spade or garden trowel, and not drawn or pulled up.

Great care must be used in planting them, to see that they are firmly set in the ground, by treading the soil firmly with the foot on each side of the plant. When planted with a dibble, after the hole is made and the plant set in it, re-enter the dibble at an angle, two or three inches from the plant, and then draw the head of the dibble sideways towards the plant, as shown in the cut on page 16. This presses the soil close up to the roots and sets the plant firmly.

The best time to transplant is on a cloudy day, just before a rain storm; but if it has to be done in bright weather, it should be done after the heat of the day is over. The plants, as removed from the seed-bed, should be placed in a pan of water, wetting their tops well. The moisture adhering to the roots when planted sufficiently moistens the soil to keep the plants from wilting. In sandy, light soils, transplanting may be done immediately after a rain storm, but in heavy soils it should be deferred until the saturation of the soil has subsided. If dry weather ensues immediately after planting, the young plants will require watering and perhaps shading, as wilting sets them back greatly.

The following table shows the number of plants that can be set on an acre of land at the various distances indicated.

NUMBER OF PLANTS REQUIRED FOR AN ACRE OF GROUND, AT THE DISTANCES INDICATED.

1	ft.	by	1	ft	43,560	4½ ft.	by	4½	ft	2,151
1½	"	by	1½	"	19,360	5	" by	1	"	8,712
2	"	by	1	"	21,780	5	" by	2	"	4,356
2	"	by	2	"	10,890	5	" by	3	"	2,904
2½	"	by	2½	"	6,961	5	" by	4	"	2,178
3	"	by	1	"	14,520	5	" by	5	"	1,742
3	"	by	2	"	7,260	5½	" by	5½	"	1,440
3	"	by	3	"	4,840	6	" by	6	"	1,210
3½	"	by	3½	"	3,555	6½	" by	6½	"	1,031
4	"	by	1	"	10,890	7	" by	7	"	888
4	"	by	2	"	5,445	8	" by	8	"	680
4	"	by	3	"	3,630	9	" by	9	"	537
4	"	by	4	"	2,722	10	" by	10	"	435

If any intermediate distances are used, the number of plants required can be ascertained by dividing 43,560, the number of square feet in an acre, by the number of square feet in the different distances. Thus, 2 feet by 2½ feet=5, and that divided into 43,560, gives 8,712, the number of plants required at the distances named.

COLD FRAMES AND HOT-BEDS.

A cold frame may be made of any size, from a one to a four sash frame. A sash is generally made six feet long, and three feet one inch wide. The stiles or side bars should each be two and a half inches wide; the parting strips of the astragals should each be half an inch wide and six inches apart, to accommodate six by eight inch glass; the thickness of the wood being an inch and a half.

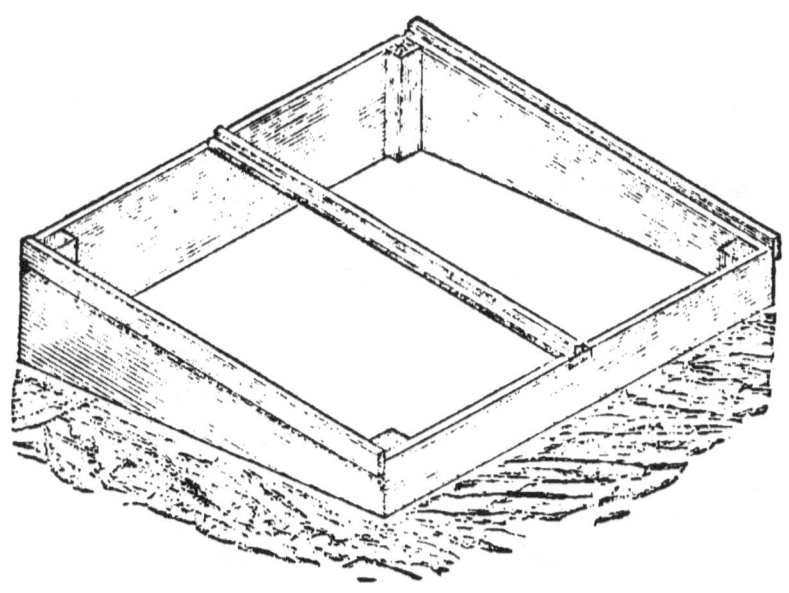

The box or frame should be two feet high at the back, and sixteen inches at the front, and should be made of inch and a half plank. When two or more sashes are used, brace-pieces six inches wide must be set across the frame, from back to front, and dovetailed into each, so as to carry the sashes and stiffen the frame. On these braces a parting-strip must be nailed, in order to separate the sashes and cause them to run true. On each side or end of the frame, a strip projecting above the ends the thickness of the sash must be nailed, to keep the sash in place.

Such a frame is usually just set on the ground in a sheltered situation, and banked up with manure, leaves, salt hay or earth to keep out the frost as much as possible.

There are two ways of making a hot-bed. One is to excavate the ground to a depth of two to two and a half feet, and the area of the frame to be used. The other is to stack the manure above ground in a square pile two and a half feet high, and about eighteen inches wider each way than the area of the frame. The first is the safest and best method.

The manure to be used should be fresh horse-dung, to which should be added, if they can be had, an equal bulk of leaves. These must be thoroughly mixed together and thrown into a conical heap, treading it down firmly as it is made up. In a few days fermentation will take place, and steam escape freely from the heap. It must now be turned over, well shaken out, and made up into a pile as before, and allowed to remain until a second fermentation takes place, which will be in three or four days. It should now be placed in the pit or piled up, as the case may be, beating it down firmly with the back of the fork, and trodden down so as to make it of uniform consistence. The frames and sashes are then to be placed upon it and banked up with manure, leaves or other suitable material, and then kept close until fermentation again ensues. In two or three days a thermometer plunged into the mass will probably indicate 100 degrees; a little air may now be given by pulling down the sashes an inch or two, and when the thermometer indicates 90 or 85 degrees, six or eight inches deep of soil should be placed over the manure. This soil should be composed of one-third well-rotted manure and two-thirds of good garden soil. In a day or two more the bed will be ready for sowing seeds in. The preparation of the bed should be so timed as to have it ready for use by the first of March.

In this bed, during the first week in March, may be sown seeds of cabbage, lettuce, peppers, egg plants and tomatoes, and any others that may be needed for early planting. The seeds should be sown in shallow drills six or eight inches apart, and covered with light soil, patting it down gently with a piece of board. When they require watering, it should be done with tepid water and given from a watering pot with a very fine rose.

After the seeds are sown, the frame should be protected at night or in dull, cold weather by coverings of wooden or straw shutters, or straw mats, so as to keep it at as near an equable temperature as possible. This must not be neglected, especially the nightly covering, until the first week in May. The bed must be kept aired in the day-time by raising or lowering the sashes whenever the thermometer shows 75 degrees, but should not be allowed to go below 68 degrees. Great attention must be paid to this, for if kept too warm, the plants will be soft and drawn, or perhaps scorched, and if too cool, will become stunted by being checked in their growth.

When the tomato, egg plant and pepper plants have grown to be two or three inches high, as many as are wanted should be transplanted, one each into three-inch pots, and set back into the frame, watering them as soon as potted, and shading them from the sun for three or four days. Cabbage and lettuce plants may be pricked out into a cold frame, and then watered and shaded as before. They should be kept as warm as possible in the cold frame, but be well aired in the middle of bright, sunny days, and will make nice, stocky plants for setting out from the middle of April to the first of May. Those wintered over in a cold frame, however, make the best plants. Tomatoes, egg plants and peppers must be kept in the hot-bed frame until the middle of May, gradually increasing the airing to keep the plants stocky.

When it is desired to raise sweet potato plants, the making of the hot-bed should be so timed as to have it ready for use by the middle of April. A compost of sand and leaf mould must be made and laid on the hot-bed six inches deep. The tubers are to be laid closely together on this, and a thickness of two inches of the compost laid evenly over them. Withhold watering them until they begin to grow. They will furnish shoots for planting out in five or six weeks after starting.

The ground, where a cold frame is to be placed in the spring, should be, the previous autumn, covered up with manure, leaves or similar materials, to keep the ground from freezing. Before setting the frame over it, it should be well spaded and made as fine as possible before setting out the plants, so that they may take root speedily after being transplanted into it.

For covering the sashes, shutters made of three-quarter inch boards should be made the size of the sashes. Or shutters may be made by making a frame of furring strips, set on edge, nailing lathes across it ten or twelve inches apart on the under side, filling it up with straw or salt hay, and then nailing a similar set of lathes on the upper side. When shutters made in either of these ways are used, strips of old carpet or canvas should be laid along the upper and lower ends of the sashes, of sufficient width to hang over the back and front of the frame, so as to cover the joint where the top and bottom rail of the sashes rest on the edges of the planks composing the frame, the object being to prevent the cold air drawing in through the joints.

Market gardeners generally use straw mats, made from rye straw, bulrushes or marsh sedge. These are best

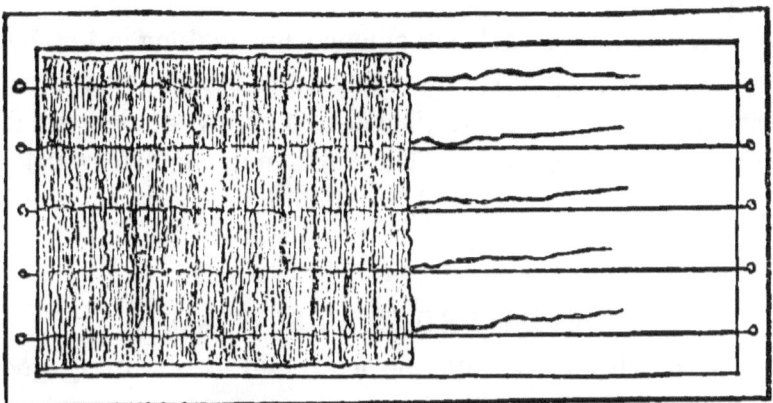

made by making a frame, the inside of which will be the width of the sash and a foot longer than it. Bore five holes in the top and bottom rails, the outside ones to be three and a half inches from the sides of the frame, and the rest eight inches apart. This will give five warp strings and make the mat the width of the sash. These warp strings, which should be of tarred string or marline, are to be fastened in the holes, and then the straw or sedge laid in small handfuls upon the lower strings; as each handful is laid on, the upper string must be carried over it and a turn taken on the lower one, and so on until the mat is finished, by tying each pair of strings together at each end. The accompanying cut will further explain this. By making it a foot longer than the sash, six inches of the mat hangs over back and front, and so saves the necessity of carpet or canvas. When finished, the mat should be about three inches thick. They are much warmer than any other covering.

Hot-beds and frames should always be protected by being placed in the angle of a close board fence, six feet high, leaving proper space to get round them. The fence should only be on the northern and western sides, so as to keep off the cold winds.

Where there is no convenience for making a hot-bed, early vegetable plants can be raised in boxes covered with loose panes of glass, and placed in a sunny window in the kitchen or sitting-room. They will not come forward as fast as those in a hot-bed, so should be started a couple of weeks sooner.

SEEDS AND SEED SOWING.

Too much care cannot be exercised in obtaining good seeds, for it is very provoking to spend money and labor upon a crop, and find that one-half or two-thirds of it is not true to name, or is of inferior quality. It makes all the difference in the world, whether we get ninety-nine good heads of cabbage out of a hundred planted, or only get ten out of a hundred, and yet we have seen such cases. Seed that may cost a dollar an ounce would, in such cases, be vastly more economical than that which only cost twenty-five cents. Always, therefore, buy the best seeds, even at a higher price, from seedsmen of established reputation.

With all the care used by seed growers and seedsmen to obtain only the best, yet sometimes disappointments will ensue, for as nearly all the vegetables we grow are monstrosities, or abnormal developments of the plants, there is a continual effort in nature to revert to the original type from whence the variety originated, and these leaps backward are sometimes very sudden. The accusations brought against seedsmen, of selling seeds that do not or will not grow, are, nine cases out of ten, perfect nonsense, as the failure to make them grow is due to the ignorance or carelessness of the cultivator. There are few vegetable seeds that do not vegetate freely when they are more than a year old, and are just as good and sometimes better than when fresh from the plant.

Those that are only considered as retaining their vitality for one year, are leeks, onions, parsnips and rhubarb.

For two years: beans and peas of all kinds, peppers, carrot, egg plant, okra, salsify, scorzonera, cress, nasturtium, thyme, sage and herb seeds generally.

For three years: artichoke, asparagus, endive, lettuce, fetticus, mustard, parsley, skirret, spinach and radish.

For four years: broccoli, cauliflower, cabbage, kale, turnip and celery.

For five years: beet, cucumber, melon, pumpkin, squash, tomato, chervil and sorrel.

The great requisites in raising plants from seeds, are a suitable soil, temperature, air and moisture. The soil should always be well pulverized and brought into fine tilth, to enable the tender, germinating plants to penetrate it. To sow seeds in heavy, coarsely broken up land, and perhaps water-soaked at that, is only labor thrown away. The temperature of the soil is a matter of great importance, and requires much discrimination, as our vegetables come from various climates, some tropical and others extra-tropical; so that a temperature that suits one would be death to the other, or will materially delay its germination. For instance, cresses will vegetate in twenty-four hours in a soil at 45 degrees. Lima beans will vegetate in seven days when the thermometer is at 83 degrees, but require twenty days if it is only at 62 degrees. Peas will vegetate in eleven days if the temperature is 74 degrees, but will require nineteen days if it is 57 degrees, and radishes will vary from six to twelve days, according to the temperature, so that no time is gained by sowing too early in the season. When seeds are sown out-of-doors, particular attention should be given so to prepare the soil as that it may become sufficiently heated by the sun's rays before the seed is sown. Attention to this point will frequently make a difference of eight to twelve days in the time of germination.

In this latitude, the following seeds may be sown from the middle of March to the end of April in the open air, the mean of the thermometer in the shade being 45 degrees. Beets, carrots, cress, celery, cabbage, cauliflower, endive, kale, kohl-rabi, lettuce, parsley, parsnip, onions, leeks, peas, radish, turnip and spinach; and the following from the middle of May to the middle of June, the mean of the thermometer being 60 degrees: lima, pole and bush beans, sweet corn, cucumber, musk and water-melons, okra, pumpkin, squash, tomato and nasturtium.

Moisture is a point that also requires much attention. If the soil is either too moist or too dry, the seeds will not vegetate. In the first case they will rot, and in the other case they will either shrivel up or remain dormant. It is difficult to explain the proper medium—that must be left to experience and common sense; but as a suggestion, we would say that when a handful of the soil is tightly pressed together in the hand, and just adheres together without becoming pasty or sticky, it is in a proper state.

Seeds will not vegetate if too much exposed to the air, and yet they must not be wholly excluded from it, as the oxygen it contains is necessary to produce those chemical changes in the seed which result in germination. Seeds **should therefore always be rolled after being sown, or the** soil be pressed in close contact with them, by laying a board over the drill, if the seeds are small, and walking on it, or if they are large, patting the soil down with the back of the spade, or pressing it down over them with the foot. This has also the effect of excluding the light, which prevents or retards their free germination.

The depth at which they are sown has also much to do in making them germinate. This is greatly controlled by the character of the soil. In stiff, clayey soils they must not be sown nearly as deep as they may be in a light, friable loam, or in a sandy soil.

The depth at which seeds should be sown is a matter for which there is no fixed rule. The old rule was, to cover them their own thickness with soil; but that is not sufficient for many seeds; cabbage seed or lettuce seed, for instance, should be sown three-eighths or half an inch deep, and peas from one to two inches. Experience and observation will soon instruct any one in this matter.

In sowing seeds in a hot-bed, great care must be had to see that the heat of the bed is at the proper temperature. If the soil of the bed is too hot, the seeds will burn up. This is a common error on the part of ignorant or injudicious gardeners, who never fail in such cases to accuse the seedsman of selling them old seed, whilst the blame for the failure rests wholly with themselves.

A certain amount of seed is necessary to produce a maximum crop; in order, therefore, to convey an approximate idea of the quantity sufficient to yield this result, and at the same time to prevent a needless waste of seed, the following Table is given, showing about the length of drill or the number of hills over which a given quantity of seed should be distributed, or the number of plants that the seed should be reasonably expected to produce.

Name of Plant.	Amount of Seed.	Average Yield.
Artichoke	1 oz	600 plants.
Asparagus	1 oz	1,000 "
Beans, English	1 qt	60 ft. of drill.
" Pole	1 qt	150 hills.
" Bush	1 qt	100 ft. of drill.
Beet	1 oz	60 " "
Borecole	1 oz	3,000 plants.
Broccoli	1 oz	3,000 "
Brussels Sprouts	1 oz	3,000 "
Cabbage	1 oz	3,000 "
Cardoon	1 oz	600 "
Carrot	1 oz	150 ft. of drill.
Cauliflower	1 oz	3,000 plants.
Celery	1 oz	4,000 "
Celeriac	1 oz	4,000 "
Chervil	1 oz	100 ft. of drill.
Chiccory	1 oz	3,000 plants.
Colewort	1 oz	3,000 "
Corn	1 qt	200 hills.
Cress	1 oz	50 ft. of drill.
Cucumber	1 oz	50 hills.
Dandelion	1 oz	4,000 plants.
Egg Plant	1 oz	2,000 "
Endive	1 oz	3,000 "
Fetticus	1 oz	100 ft. of drill.
Garden Patience	1 oz	600 plants.
Kohl-Rabi	1 oz	3,000 "
Leek	1 oz	1,500 "
Lettuce	1 oz	3,000 "
Martynia	1 oz	500 "
Melons	1 oz	60 hills.
Mustard	1 oz	50 ft. of drill.
Nasturtium	1 oz	100 plants.
New Zealand Spinach	1 oz	50 "
Okra	1 oz	40 ft. of drill.
Onion	1 oz	100 " "
Onion Sets	1 qt	20 " "
Parsley	1 oz	150 " "

Name of Plant.	Amount of Seed.	Average Yield.
Parsnip	1 oz	200 ft. of drill.
Peas	1 qt	100 " "
Peppers	1 oz	2,000 plants.
Potatoes	10 bush. sets	1 acre.
Pumpkin	1 oz	40 hills.
Radish	1 oz	100 ft. of drill.
Rhubarb	1 oz	500 plants.
Ruta-Baga	1 oz	200 ft. of drill.
Salsify	1 oz	70 " "
Scolymus	1 oz	70 " "
Scorzonera	1 oz	70 " "
Sea-Kale	1 oz	30 " "
Shallot	1 qt	20 " "
Sorrel	1 oz	600 plants.
Spinach	1 oz	150 ft. of drill.
Squash, Bush	1 oz	50 hills.
" Running	1 oz	16 "
Sweet Potato	½ pk	12 bushels.
Swiss Chard	1 oz	50 ft. of drill.
Tomato	1 oz	2,000 plants.
Water-Melon	1 oz	30 hills.

PROTECTING VEGETABLES.

When cauliflowers, tomatoes and other tender vegetables are set out early in the season, it is frequently necessary to protect them not only from cold nights, but from chilly, windy days, for we are seldom certain of really settled, warm weather, until the last week of May or beginning of June; and although there may not be any frost, yet the chill the plants get, causes them to become stunted and retards their growth.

If it is only necessary to protect them when first set out, to prevent them wilting or to guard them against frost at night, an inverted flower-pot will answer every purpose; taking it off during the day when the plants have recovered from being transplanted, and replacing it at night, or keeping it over them if the day should be chilly or windy. When it is necessary not only to protect them but to increase the temperature, they may be protected by covering them with small boxes eight or ten inches square, made higher at the back than the front, like a small cold frame; and a pane of 6x8 or 10x12 glass let in the top, according to the size of the frame. The frame may be made of thin boards, and need not be over a foot high at the back.

The following is a very simple and excellent plan for protecting freshly set out melons, cucumbers, squashes and similar plants from cool winds, and, when growing, from the attacks of bugs. The forkful of manure usually applied to each hill is first dug into the soil. A seven-inch flower-pot is then placed upon the hill, and the earth drawn round it with a hoe and firmly trodden with the foot. The flower-pot is then withdrawn, and the seeds are sown or the plant set out in the bottom of the cavity thus made. Our

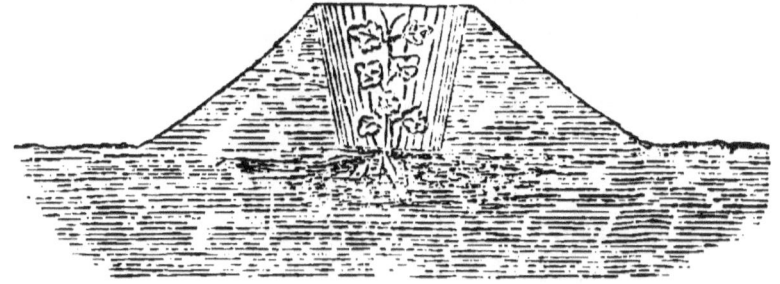

engraving fully explains how this is done. The vine, when sufficiently grown, runs down the sides of the mound, whilst the stem and roots are kept cooler and more moist than when surrounded with boxes of wood or similar contrivances. Plants thus set out can also be readily protected from late frosts or cold rains or winds, by simply placing a pane of 8x10 glass or a piece of board of similar size over the hole, at night or during the prevalence of the injurious weather.

PRESERVATION OF VEGETABLES.

In our directions for the cultivation of vegetables, we have given instructions for their preservation whenever any special mode of doing so was deemed necessary; we shall therefore here only give general directions for so doing.

All root crops, such as beets, carrots, parsnips, turnips, potatoes, horseradish, etc., are better preserved in outdoor pits than in cellars, as they keep more plump and succulent, and have less tendency to become stringy than when kept in a cellar. Besides this it is more healthful thus to keep them than in a cellar, for unless care is taken to remove any that may decay, they are liable to produce disease among those living in the house. Only so many ought to be thus kept as will supply the family for three or four weeks.

In a dry, sheltered situation, dig out a series of shallow pits a foot deep, and of such length and width as may be necessary for the bulk of each vegetable to be preserved. Into each pit place the roots, they having been previously topped, and pile them up in a rounding manner. On them lay three or four inches of straw or leaves, and over this place a layer of soil eighteen or twenty inches deep, beating it down firmly with the back of the spade, and sloping it off nicely. Cover the southerly end of each pit with a thick layer of leaves, straw or litter, to keep the soil from freezing, and to afford ready access to them during the hard winter weather. If there is any danger of water lodging in the pits, drains must be dug in such a manner as to readily carry it off. If old boards or fence rails can be had, a pent house roof, like a chicken coop, can be made over each pit, and the earth laid on it, and the straw or litter be omitted. The best time for doing this is towards the end of November or the first of December.

Cabbages are best preserved by pulling them up by the roots, and placing them head down on a level piece of dry ground, and then throwing six or seven inches of earth over them.

A portion of the stalks will be exposed, but this is of no importance; the spaces between them can be filled up with leaves or litter, which will facilitate getting them out when wanted.

Cauliflowers and broccoli that have not perfected their heads in the autumn, should be taken up and planted close together right up to the leaves, in a cold frame, and protected by sashes and coverings. They will then perfect their flower-heads. Onions are best preserved by laying them on the floor of a hay-loft and covering them with about a foot or eighteen inches of hay or straw. They require to be kept dry and cool.

SEED RAISING.

As a rule it is not best for an amateur gardener to raise seeds for his own use, as the business requires much skill and knowledge, and is best conducted by those who make a regular business of it. Even seedsmen rarely grow seeds for their own sales, but purchase them from growers, many of whom make specialties of different kinds, some only growing one particular sort of cabbage, spinach, lettuce, etc., and others only growing other varieties of the same vegetable.

The reason for this is that the various varieties of any one vegetable are liable to mix if grown in proximity to each other; for instance, if any two varieties of cabbage, or of beets, or of lettuce, or of melons, are grown within a quarter of a mile of each other, their pollen will be liable to be blown by the wind, or carried by bees or other insects from one plot to the other, and produce cross fertilization, which will result in the production of mongrels, none of which are likely to have any of the distinguishing characteristics of their parents. It is, therefore, best to buy what seeds are needed from seedsmen of well-established reputation, whose knowledge of their business, and of the growers, generally enables them to be certain of their purity. Seedsmen, as a rule, always endeavor to get the best they can, and often pay extraordinary prices for them, as their gardener customers are always ready to pay an extra price for the very best, for it is a matter of great importance to them, especially to market gardeners, to be sure to obtain a crop to pay for the great outlay for the manure and labor necessary in their cultivation.

If any of our readers should, however, desire to grow seeds for their own use, they should observe the following rules:

Never to grow for seed any two varieties of any given vegetable, for the reasons already given.

In the case of vegetables desirable for their earliness, as tomatoes, melons, cucumbers, etc., always to save the fruits first ripe, if they are perfect in other particulars.

In the case of beets, carrots and other tap-rooted or tuberous-rooted vegetables, always select the best formed and the best colored roots, being careful to so dig them up as not to destroy or injure the tips of the roots, and always to leave an inch at least of the tops on the roots, for if cut down close to the crown, they will be injured for seed-growing purposes. The largest and best formed potatoes should always be saved for cutting into sets, as the small ones, which are too often saved for this purpose, are the last formed in the ground, and are not as well ripened as the large ones, which are first formed and have had a longer season in which to perfect themselves.

All the annual vegetables, such as beans, corn, cucumbers, egg plants, peppers, tomatoes, radishes, peas, melons, etc., produce their seeds the same season as that in which they are planted.

The biennial vegetables, such as beets, carrots, celery, cabbage, onions, leeks, parsley, salsify, scorzonera, parsnips, etc., produce their seeds the second year after they are planted, and are raised from roots or plants that have been wintered over. Set them out as early in the spring as the weather permits, setting them the same distance apart as is directed for growing them.

INSECTS AND INSECTICIDES.

If a garden is kept well cultivated by having the soil frequently stirred by the hoe, it will not be much troubled by insects, as many of them go into the ground in their pupa state to winter over. The continual digging for the various crops as they succeed each other also destroys them. Nevertheless, there are some which, under almost any circumstances, will annoy the cultivator. One of the most troublesome on newly turned up grass land is the white grub with a black head, the larva of the June bug, or cockchafer. This grub is very voracious, and eats off young cabbage plants and others almost as soon as they are planted. It is difficult to get rid of them, as they are underground. Their ravages are done at night, and the grub may be found early in the morning, by digging for them within two or three inches of the plant gnawed off.

Moles are particularly destructive to these grubs, as they feed upon them. Here we would say a word in favor of the mole, who is popularly but ignorantly accused of eating the roots of vegetables. On the contrary, he is an insectivorous or carnivorous animal, and does not live on vegetables. He burrows through the ground seeking his prey, and is one of the best friends the gardener has. The only mischief he does is under-running a plant now and then when burrowing, but the chances are ten to one that he has caught and devoured the grub that was eating it off, and which, had he not done so, would have devoured a dozen more plants.

The most general insects in a vegetable garden are the aphis, or plant louse, caterpillars of various kinds, some bugs, slugs, and plant fleas.

The aphis are readily destroyed by dipping the shoots of the plants in a strong decoction or tea made from tobacco stems. The smooth-skinned caterpillars, particularly the species which infests the cabbage, may be destroyed by sprinkling salt upon them. Bugs or beetles are not always destructive, for some of the ground beetles live upon other insects; those that feed upon plants are generally easily killed by sprinkling the plants with a solution of whale oil soap. Some of them, such as the squash bug, can be kept from the plants by enclosing them with old cheese boxes or similar arrangements. The insect cannot fly but an inch or two from the ground, and when the plant is thus defended cannot get at it. Fleas, such as the turnip fly or flea, can be kept in check by dusting the soil with lime, repeating it every day or two, until the plants are well up. For the Colorado bug, which of late years has been so destructive to the potato, nothing is better to destroy it than Paris green. This should be mixed with plenty of water, kept stirred, and sprinkled on the plants with a whisk broom or some similar article.

Tobacco water, tobacco dust, soot, lime, hellebore powder, dry guano, flour of sulphur, whale oil soap, and solutions of saltpetre or salt are all insecticides. They must be cautiously used; their strength being graduated when used in solution, according to the plant, and the insects to be destroyed. This is best ascertained by actual experiment.

Insectivorous birds, lady bugs and toads are great devourers of insects, and should always be encouraged in a garden. The birds not only devour the living insects, but also devour the insect eggs, of which they are very fond. Lady bugs live upon the plant lice, and toads live upon small winged insects, of which they catch large numbers.

CULTIVATION OF VEGETABLES.

The preceding pages are devoted solely to the most practical and economical methods of preparing a garden for the reception and culture of vegetables, etc., with such general remarks on the tillage of the soil, the rotation of crops, and other matters connected with the subject, as will ensure the most favorable results.

The present portion of the work will afford thorough information as to the most approved manner of sowing, planting and cultivating all the plants that find a place in a vegetable garden.

Each will be treated separately, and the whole is arranged in alphabetical order for handy reference. There is also introduced, at the end of the book, a monthly Reminder, or general summary of the planting and other work which is appropriate or necessary during each month.

ARTICHOKE.

Artichoke plants can be raised either from seeds, from suckers, or from offshoots of old plants. The seed should be sown toward the end of March or during April, in any light, moist earth, not liable to bake, nor yet very sandy. The seed drills should be about an inch deep and twelve inches apart. A bed will last three or four years, and one ounce of seed should produce about six hundred plants. The *Green Globe* is the best (because the hardiest) variety for our climate. When the plants are about nine or ten inches high they should be transplanted into the bed in which they are to be permanently grown, taking advantage of cloudy or wet weather for this operation. As the roots penetrate to a great depth and the plants require very rich soil, the bed should be heavily manured, well and deeply spaded, and the soil well pulverized. A good dressing of salt, as for asparagus, is also useful—for the artichoke likes a saline soil—and a top dressing of it may also be given every year or two.

After being carefully taken up, the plants may be set with a dibble, in rows four or five feet apart and two feet from plant to plant on the row; being careful not to insert the heart of the leaves below the surface of the soil. If the weather is dry at the time of planting, or should be dry before the plants get well established, liberal watering should be given. In a bed composed of seedlings there will often be found a great difference in the size of the flower buds or heads—the part used. It is therefore best to mark those which produce the largest and most succulent flower heads, and from these take the suckers for planting a new bed. These should be taken off in May, when they are five or six inches high, and planted in a permanent bed prepared as above directed.

The after culture consists in keeping the bed clear of weeds and every season spading in some manure in order to produce healthy, vigorous plants, with strong flower stalks and blooms. Unless wanted for the purpose of making a new bed in the spring, all the suckers, with the exception of two or three, should be taken off the parent plant, in order to strengthen it. The object to be attained is large flower heads—hence the whole culture must be such as will produce a strong growth of the plants, giving them plenty of room to develop their foliage and sustaining the plants with liberal supplies of manure. If the flower stems show more than three or four flower buds, all in excess of that number should be removed. In winter, when the frost sets in, the plants should each receive a covering five or six inches thick, of leaves, sea-weed, or long manure, to protect them from frost. If there is any probability of water lodging on the bed during winter, then drains of a foot or more in depth should be dug about two feet from the rows, so as to carry off the water, for, by lodging on the plants, it will cause the crowns to rot.

When grown for chard the leaves and flower stalks should be cut off in June or early in July, within six inches of the ground. In September or October, when the new leaves are about two feet long, they should be somewhat loosely tied together and wound with hay or straw bands to blanch them, adding some litter at the bottom to assist the process; or they may be earthed up in the same way as celery. In about six weeks they will be ready for use. This blanching process should only be done with old beds about to be broken up, as it destroys the plants for blooming. When it is intended to use the heads for pickling they should be cut when about two inches in diameter. When they are to be used as salad, cut them when they have nearly attained their full size, but before the scales of the calyx begin to open or spread. When the receptacles or bottoms are to be used for stewing or frying, the heads should be cut just as the scales begin to spread or open. If they are allowed to remain until the flower proper begins to show itself, they become unfit for use.

ASPARAGUS.

This plant will succeed in any rich, deep, dry and porous soil, through which water can readily drain away; but it does not succeed well in heavy, close soils deficient in under drainage; but if this latter requisite is provided, almost any soil can be so prepared as to produce fair crops of it.

Asparagus plants are raised by sowing the seeds in the month of September if autumn sown, or in the month of April if spring sown. The seed bed should be composed of good, rich soil, well pulverized and manured with well-rotted manure. The seed, of which an ounce will produce about a thousand plants, or be sufficient for fifty or sixty feet of drill, should be thinly sown in drills twelve inches apart and an inch in depth. After the plants come up, the bed should be kept thoroughly clear of weeds by repeated hoeings. The plants, if well cared for, will be large enough to plant out in permanent beds when a year old, but some cultivators prefer to let them remain until they are two years old. Ordinarily it is a saving of time to purchase the roots from a nurseryman or seedsman, as one or two years' time can be gained by so doing.

As asparagus beds, if properly prepared and attended to, will yield good shoots for twenty years, it is poor policy to neglect the proper preparation of the bed, or stint the supply of fertilizing material. They may be prepared and planted either in the autumn or in the spring as soon as the ground is in good working order, up to the middle or end of April. The ground should be trenched two spades deep, and each spade of depth should have three or four inches deep of well-rotted manure dug into the soil, mixing it thoroughly. Coarse bone-dust or crushed bone is also an excellent fertilizer for this plant.

It is usual to plant the roots in beds each five feet wide, and containing three rows of plants one foot apart and a foot between either of the outer rows and the edge of the bed, and then allowing two or two and a half feet alleyway between the beds; but this is by no means absolutely necessary, as the beds can be made of any desired width, and we think it is better to give greater space between the rows than is usually done—say fifteen to eighteen inches apart—in order to allow free access of light and air, for it is the strong, healthy growth of the plant during the present season, that produces a crop of large, succulent shoots the ensuing spring and summer.

Another mode is to plant them in long rows three feet apart, with the plants set fifteen to eighteen inches apart on the row; preparing the soil with the plow and subsoiler, working in plenty of manure into the trenches. This is the mode adopted for field culture, and where the garden space admits of it, and the beds are cultivated by horse hoes, it is the preferable mode if large quantities of shoots are required.

In planting the roots after the beds are prepared, stretch a line the length of the row, open a trench six or eight inches deep, somewhat sloping on the side next to the line, against this side lay the plants with the crowns about six or seven inches from the surface of the bed, spreading out the roots fanwise, and as you proceed throwing in the excavated earth against them, and pressing it down firmly with the foot. When planted in rows a foot apart the plants will get more air and light by being planted in quincunx.

The after cultivation of the beds consists in keeping them scrupulously clear of weeds; every spring give them a top dressing of rotted manure, superphosphate of lime or guano. In the interior of the country, away from the influence of the sea air, a top dressing of salt is beneficial, applied at the rate of fifteen or sixteen pounds to sixty square yards. A liberal application of liquid manure may also be used to great advantage. A spading fork is proferable to a spade in turning in the manure, as it is less liable to cut or injure the roots, but even this should not be inserted more than five or six inches deep. In sections of the country where the winters are severe, or there is but little snow, it is prudent to protect the beds by a covering of leaves, sea-weed, or long manure, three or four inches thick, removing it early in the spring.

The shoots should not be cut before the third year after planting, and then but sparingly; after that the yield will be abundant. In the Middle States the cutting should cease about the 10th of June, but in the Eastern and Northern States it may be continued until the 25th of that month. All the shoots that form seed berries should be cut out as soon as the berries are formed, or the berries stripped off, as the seed bearing is very exhaustive to the plant, and causes the roots to send up weak shoots the next season.

A bed containing about thirty square yards will supply from twenty-five to thirty shoots a day.

All of the so-called varieties of asparagus appear to be but one, except, perhaps, the variety known as *Conover's Colossal*. Good cultivation produces all the distinction that there is between them.

ENGLISH BROAD BEANS.

This class of beans is largely grown in England and Scotland, but in this country it does not succeed so well, on account of the excessive heat. If, however, they are sown very early in the open ground, or started in pots or boxes in a frame or cellar and transplanted, a good crop may be had in June. They require a cool, humid climate, and strong, moist soil moderately enriched; if the soil is light, it should be manured freely with cow manure. Outdoor sowing should be done as soon in the spring as the ground is in working order.

They should be sown in drills about two inches deep, but varying as to the distance of the rows and the plants on the row, according to the variety. When they are three or four inches high they should be carefully hoed, and as they progress should be earthed up once or twice during their growth. When the young pods form on the lower part of the stem, the top shoots should be pinched off; otherwise the plant will go on growing and flowering, to the injury and retardation of the crop. They may be greatly forwarded by starting them in a moderate hot-bed in February, and transplanting them out-of-doors about the 20th of March, or from that time until the first of April, according to the weather. The transplanting should be carefully done with a trowel, so as not to check their growth.

Another mode is to cover a small piece of ground in the autumn with a sufficient thickness of manure or leaves to keep out the frost, removing the covering in February, and then placing a frame and sashes over the soil and sowing the seeds in it. The frame must be protected from frost by suitable coverings to the sashes, and banking up the frame with earth or manure. The seeds may also be sown in February in pots or boxes in a light, warm cellar, keeping them close to the windows. The plants raised by either of these modes are to be transplanted as already directed. The pods should be gathered for use when the beans are half grown, as they are then delicate in flavor, while if allowed to grow larger they become coarse flavored, flatulent and indigestible.

Many varieties are grown abroad, but for our climate

the three following are the best: *Marshall's Early Dwarf Prolific*, which grows from eighteen inches to two feet high, branching out very freely at the bottom, and is very productive (the rows should be two and a half to three feet apart, with the plants four to six inches apart on the row); the *Royal Dwarf Cluster*, which grows only ten to fifteen inches high, is very productive and branches considerably (the rows should be eighteen to twenty inches apart, and the plants ten to twelve inches apart on the row); and the *Long Pod*, which grows from three to four feet high, is non-branching and very productive, but later than the first two varieties named. The rows of *Long Pod* should be three to four feet apart, and the plants four to six inches apart on the row.

BUSH BEANS.

These will grow in any good garden soil moderately enriched; if too highly manured it will cause them to run to tops too much. The proper time for sowing them is from any period after the 10th of May until the beginning of August. It is better to sow them in drills than in hills; the drills should be about two inches deep, and from two to three feet apart, according to the sort. The beans should be dropped from two to three inches apart on the row. As they progress in growth, hoe them carefully, and draw up some earth to the stems.

The varieties are very numerous, but for ordinary cultivation the following three sorts will be quite sufficient:

Early Valentine; is early, tender and productive, generally being fit for use six weeks after sowing. It continues much longer in a green state than most other varieties.

Newington Wonder; is a very dwarf growing variety and wonderfully productive. The pods are very tender. It is an excellent succession sort. The drills for this sort may be two feet apart.

Refugee; is a very productive, but not an early sort; the pods are tender, of good flavor, and much used for pickling. It withstands the late heats of summer better than most other sorts.

POLE BEANS.

There are two classes of these beans—those which are used as string beans and those which are used as shelled beans. The former are scarcely worth the trouble of growing, as their place is well supplied by the dwarf string beans, which are much easier grown.

They require a light, somewhat sandy soil, which must be well enriched with manure in the hills in which they are grown. The seeds should be sown about two inches deep in hills three to four feet apart, with a stake or pole eight or nine feet high set in the centre of the hill at the time of planting. The planting should not be done before the 15th of May and may be continued until the end of June. If planted too early they will rot in the ground. Five or six beans should be sown in each hill, and when they have attained their second leaf, all but three or four should be pulled up. The after cultivation consists in one or two hillings up and keeping them clear of weeds. Nipping off the ends of the shoots after they have reached the top of the poles has a tendency to make the plants more fruitful.

If it is desired to have them earlier than they would produce in the open air, plants can be raised from beans sown one each in a half pint pot in April and kept in a cold frame; these will be ready for transplanting by the end of May, and will come in ten days or two weeks sooner than those sown in the open air.

Of those used as string beans the *London Horticultural* is the best, as it can also be used as a shelled bean, and is excellent when dried or ripe.

Of the shelled class none equals the *Lima* and its variety, the *Siera*. The latter is somewhat hardier and is several days earlier than the first, but is not so large.

BEET.

Beets require a rich, deep, well-pulverized soil; but it is not necessary to manure the soil for the present crop if it has been well manured for previous crops of other vegetables. Coarse manure produces misshapen, ill-flavored roots. A top dressing of salt or guano, bone dust, superphosphate or wood ashes, is beneficial, even if the soil is rich.

For an early crop the turnip-rooted varieties are the most suitable. They can be sown as early as the first week of April in a sheltered border. The drills should be a foot apart and one to two inches in depth; the seeds being dropped along the row about two inches apart, then covered in with a rake, and rolled or else pressed down by laying a board over the drill and walking on it, to set the earth firmly about the seeds. For succession crops, sow every two weeks, from the first of April until the first of June. The crop will be more tender and delicate when thus sown in succession, as those first sown become harder and not so well flavored as the hot weather approaches.

When the plants are three or four inches high, they should be thinned out to six inches apart. As each capsule contains five or six seeds, as many plants will come up from each, thus making several plants have the appearance of one. It is therefore necessary to carefully thin out each little group to one plant, as otherwise they will interfere with and choke each other. This thinning out should be done when the plants are quite young. If any vacancies occur in the bed, dibble in some of the plants drawn out, being careful not to break the tips of the roots. During their growth they require to be frequently hoed and to be kept clear of weeds.

The general crop of long-rooted varieties should be sown about the end of May, or during June, as the plants will then have a free, unchecked growth, which prevents the roots becoming tough or stringy through being stunted. Even if sown as late as the first week in July, they will frequently produce good roots in the autumn. The rows should be from eighteen inches to two feet apart, and the plants eight or ten inches apart on the row. The after culture consists in keeping them well hoed and free from weeds.

A dozen or more varieties may be found in the seed catalogues, but the following three, all things considered, are the best:

Egyptian Turnip-rooted; this is the earliest variety; it has small upright leaves; the roots are of a deep crimson color, and well flavored.

Early Short Top Round; is an improvement on the *Early Blood Turnip-rooted;* it is shorter in the leaves, more free from rootlets, and flatter in shape.

Long Smooth Blood; is earlier than the common blood, is not so strong a grower, and more free from rootlets.

BORECOLE OR KALE.

Of this vegetable there are two classes—one grown for spring use, and the other for autumn and winter use.

The first, known as dwarf German greens, and in our markets as sprouts, should be sown somewhat thinly in drills half an inch deep and a foot apart, in the month of September; the beds in which it remains receiving the same treatment as spinach. It requires a good rich, light soil, well drained, for if water lodges on the beds it will rot.

Those for autumn use should be sown in seed beds from the middle of April to the middle of May, and transplanted into the permanent bed in June or July. They also require a good rich soil, their cultivation in all respects being the same as that of cabbage. They are very hardy, and are better flavored when touched by frost than otherwise.

The best two varieties for winter use are the *Dwarf Green Curled* and the *Purple Leaved*. The first seldom grows more than eighteen inches high, and the plants may be set that distance apart. The last grows about thirty inches high, and should be planted two feet apart on the rows.

BROCCOLI.

This vegetable is so similar to, and so closely allied to the cauliflower, that it is almost impossible for those not having a botanical education to see wherein the difference consists, yet from certain botanical distinctions they may be distinguished one from the other. The broccoli is generally supposed to have been derived from the tall curled kale, and originated in the northern part of Europe, whilst the cauliflower is supposed to have been derived from what is known as the *Couve Tronchuda*, or *Portugal Cabbage*, and to have originated in the south of Europe; tradition says in the Isle of Cyprus. The broccoli is much the hardier of the two, and is best for an autumn crop in this country.

Broccoli requires a very rich soil, its general treatment being the same as cabbage. A top dressing of lime and salt, or a mulching of sea-weed, is very useful to them. The seed should be sown in a seed bed in the open air about the middle of May, rather sparingly in drills half an inch deep, and from four to six inches apart. A quarter of an ounce of seed will sow a piece of ground four by four feet, and produce about a thousand plants.

The plants will be of proper size to transplant by the beginning of July, when they should be set out in a permanent bed, giving them a good watering after they have been transplanted. The proper distance to set them is in rows two and a half feet apart, and the plants two feet apart on the rows. After they have well taken root, they should have a good deep hoeing, and this should be repeated two or three times, as they progress in growth, drawing up some earth to the stems at each hoeing.

Every care should be had not to allow the plants to become stunted by the extreme heat or drought of the summer; to produce good flower heads, they require to be kept in a growing, flourishing condition until the commencement of cool, moist autumn weather. Frequent waterings may therefore be necessary, should the summer be hot or dry; occasional waterings with manure water will be very beneficial under any circumstances.

Under almost any circumstances it will be found that some of the plants will not flower before frost sets in.

Such plants should be carefully lifted and planted up to their leaves, just close enough together to touch each other, in a frame two boards high, banked up with earth, manure or leaves, covered with sashes, protecting them from the frost at night or on cold days with suitable coverings of straw or hay, giving air in the middle of the day on fine, sunny days. If there is an overplus of heads, they may be saved by lifting the plants and planting them in boxes filled with earth, and placed in a light, dry cellar.

Out of more than a hundred varieties known in England, the following three varieties will be found the most satisfactory to the amateur grower in this country. *Purple Cape*, a very hardy, sure heading variety, with purple flower heads; the color disappears in cooking, and it does not differ from the white variety in flavor. *Early Walcheren*, by some considered a cauliflower, has white flower heads, and is much earlier than the other varieties. It is the leading variety among market gardeners.

Knight's Protecting; is a very hardy white flowered variety, of dwarf, compact growth; the plants may therefore be set eighteen inches apart in the row. It is not an early variety, but is excellent for planting in frames, as it will continue heading until January.

BRUSSELS SPROUTS.

This delicious vegetable belongs to the cabbage family and in its general appearance resembles a tall kale or borecole. It grows three or four feet high, producing on the stem numerous miniature cabbage heads, varying from one to two inches in diameter, which are very tender and delicately flavored, especially when slightly touched by frost.

The seed should be sown about the middle of May in a prepared bed, and in July the plants should be transplanted two feet each way in the permanent bed, or the seeds may be sown in a hot-bed in March or April, and the plants transplanted when three or four inches high, which will bring them into use a month or six weeks earlier than when sown in May. The after culture is the same as that of cabbages.

If the later planted plants should not head, they should be taken up before severe freezing weather sets in, and planted in a cellar, when they will afford a succession of heads during the winter.

The tall or giant variety is the hardiest, and produces the largest number of heads. As this vegetable is apt to revert back to its original type, and not to produce its small heads unless great care is used in saving the seed, it should only be purchased from seedsmen of known respectability.

CABBAGE.

Cabbage requires a deep, fresh, loamy soil, and does not succeed well in land that has been long under cultivation, or that is very dry and sandy.

The soil in which it is grown should be liberally manured, especially for the early varieties, with good barn-yard manure, and as it likes a limestone and saline soil, an addition of fine ground bone, and a top dressing of salt, will be found advantageous, or manure prepared with the lime and salt mixture as directed in the chapter on Manures. Wood ashes are also useful.

There are two or three ways of raising the early sorts. The first mode is to sow the seeds in an open-air prepared bed, from the 10th to the 25th of September, and, when the plants are five or six weeks old, pricking them out into a cold frame three to six inches apart each way, inserting the plant down to the first leaf, and then protecting them during the winter by sashes and straw or litter coverings, giving them plenty of air on bright, sunny days. Plants thus raised make very hardy, stocky plants for spring planting.

Another mode is in the fall to set a frame in a warm, sheltered situation, and filling it up with leaves, and then covering it with sashes or boards, and over them straw or leaves, to prevent the frost from getting down to the soil. About the latter end of January or beginning of February the leaves may be thrown out, the soil nicely dug, and the seed sown in the frame, putting on the sashes and protecting it from the frost as in the first mode.

The third mode is to sow the seed in a hot-bed about the latter end of February or the beginning of March. For their general treatment in this mode, see the chapter on Hot-beds.

From the first to the middle of April, the plants raised by either of these modes may be transplanted with a dibble into the permanent bed, and will produce good heads in June. The distance apart will depend upon the varieties grown, some requiring much more room than others, as they differ in their growths. Such early sorts as we shall recommend may be planted in rows two feet apart, the plants being set on the rows eighteen inches apart. They should be occasionally hoed and earthed up.

For the late or autumn crop, the seed should be sown in a prepared bed in the open ground during the month of May, the drills being three or four inches apart. In all sowings, see that the plants do not stand too thickly together, so as to guard against their being drawn up. In the second or third week of July they should be transplanted into the permanent bed, in rows three feet apart, and two feet from plant to plant. As they progress in growth, they should receive three or four deep hoeings and be slightly earthed up.

For the different ways of preserving cabbage during the winter, see the chapter on Preserving Vegetables.

Cabbage is very liable to be what is called club-footed, when grown two or more years in succession on the same soil; it should therefore always be grown succeeding peas, beets, carrots, parsnips, or some other crop dissimilar to itself, and never after cauliflowers, kohl-rabi, German greens, or any other cruciferous plants. This disease shows itself in the form of radish-like swellings of the stem or of knotty protuberances on the roots, and is generally discernible on the young plants in the seed bed at the time of transplanting. All such plants should be thrown away. Soil has much to do with clubbing, which is more prevalent on poor, gravelly soils, than upon those that are deep and rich. Some persons think that the disease is due to the larvæ of an insect, as the grub of some insect is almost always found in the diseased part, but insects being found in these abnormal growths is not always proof that the insects have produced them, for many insects seek such growths in which to lay their eggs. Others think that it is due to the exhaustion from the soil of some constituent necessary to the growth of the plant. We know that all the cabbage tribe have a large quantity of sulphur in their composition, as is evidenced by the fumes of sulphureted hydrogen given out when they are in a state of fermentation and decomposition, and the flour made from the seed, as in flour of mustard, turning silver black when exposed to its action. It may therefore be that this element may be largely wanting in some soils, and soon exhausted by the cabbage crop. Late experiments in England bear out this view, as it has been found that a light sprinkling of flour of sulphur in the seed drills, or sulphur applied with the manure at the rate of seven or eight pounds to the acre, is a preventive of this disease. It would also destroy the larvæ of the insect if it is caused by it, as no insects can stand the action of sulphur, which, in a finely comminuted state, is no doubt readily acted upon by the atmosphere, and flour of sulphur always contains a large amount of free sulphurous acid gas.

The varieties of cabbage are very numerous, but for family use the following sorts will be found the most desirable. The large, coarse-headed sorts are by no means the best, as they are wanting in delicacy of flavor, and are only suitable for farming purposes or for making sauerkraut.

Early Jersey Wakefield; for an early cabbage has a large sized head, with small outside leaves, and heads well. As it does not produce seed freely, it is sometimes difficult to get seeds of this sort. It is so much esteemed by the New York market gardeners, that they sometimes pay $20 per pound for the seed.

Early York; is an old standard sort, very productive, and quite as early as the preceding, but not as large headed. It is a compact growing sort, and may be planted in rows eighteen inches apart, and fifteen to eighteen inches in the rows.

Bergen Drumhead: is one of the most popular sorts grown for the New York market, producing large, round, tender and well flavored heads. It should be planted three feet apart each way.

Mason; is a New England variety of medium size, forming a solid head; it is very reliable in heading and is very fine flavored.

Green Globe Savoy; has a medium sized, round but rather loosely formed head of fine texture, and excellent, mild flavor. The inner loose leaves are nearly as good as the head when cooked. It is very hardy, and is better for use after it has been frosted. As it is late in heading, it should be sown early in the seed bed.

Red Dutch; is chiefly used for pickling, or for mixing with white cabbage, in making cold-slaw. It has a medium sized, very solid head of a deep red color, and keeps well. Like the savoys, it takes a long season to mature, and should therefore be sown early.

CARDOON.

This plant belongs to the same genus as the artichoke; the stems of the leaves, which are thick and crisp, being used when blanched as asparagus or celery, for soups, stews, or as a salad. It is in season in autumn and early winter.

It requires a moderately rich soil, enriched with well-decomposed manure; if the manure is too fresh and strong, the plants will be apt to run to seed, when it becomes useless as a vegetable.

The seeds should be sown in April, in rows three feet apart, in groups of three or four seeds, the groups being twelve or fifteen inches apart on the row, and the seeds covered an inch or an inch and a half deep. When the plants are three or four inches high, all but one in each group should be pulled up. If during the summer the weather should be very dry, they should be freely watered.

In September the plants will have attained their full growth and be ready for blanching. This process is best done by tying the leaves together with bast matting or string, then drawing a little earth up to the base of the plant, and then covering it vertically, or thatching it with a thickness of one or two inches of long straw, held in place by proper ties of matting or twine. In about three or four weeks they will be sufficiently blanched to use.

For a winter supply, the plants may be laid in a trench as directed for celery, or taken up with their roots just before cold weather sets in, and then packed in dry sand, one course above another, in a dry cellar. They will keep well and become more perfectly blanched.

There are five or six sorts, but for use in this country the *Large Smooth* is as good as any.

CARROT.

The carrot prefers a light, loamy soil, that has been well manured for the previous crops and does not require fresh manure; for if the soil is too rich, the plants have a tendency to run to leaf and not to form roots, and fresh manure is apt to cause the roots, as it does with all spindle-shaped roots, to become forked and deformed. The soil should be deeply spaded and well pulverized.

For an early crop, a small bed may be sown in a sheltered spot as early as the end of March, and from that time until the end of May, at intervals of two weeks, for succession crops. The principal or late crop should not be sown until June.

For the early crop the drills should be about an inch deep and a foot apart, the plants being thinned out to five or six inches apart on the row, and kept well hoed and clear of weeds during the season. When grown as a field crop, the drills should be twenty inches apart. As the seed comes up slowly, and does not mark out the row very distinctly, a sprinkling of red turnip-rooted radish is often sown in the same drills with the carrot seed, in order to facilitate the hoeing and weeding. Owing to the seed being liable to be killed by drought, it is always best to sow it somewhat thickly, and thin out afterwards. The soil should always be rolled after the seed is sown, so as to firm it down and keep the dry summer air from the seed, as that retards and even prevents its vegetating.

The best two sorts for garden culture, are the

Early Horn, which is best for the early crop; the root is about two inches in diameter and six inches in length, tapering but little and terminating abruptly in a very slender tap-root. On account of its short root, it is well adapted for thin, poor soils, in which the longer rooted varieties do not succeed so well. In such soils it can be grown as a late as well as an early crop.

The *Long Orange* is generally grown for the main crop, and is so well known that it does not need any description. It is as well adapted for field as for garden culture.

CAULIFLOWER.

Like the broccoli, to which it is akin, the cauliflower requires a very rich soil to succeed well and to grow it to perfection. In our climate it is best grown for early summer use, as it does not succeed as well as the broccoli when grown for autumn use, owing to the severe heat and drought of our summers.

The best mode of cultivating it, is to sow the seeds, from the 10th to the 20th of September, in a bed of rich soil. In from four to six weeks afterwards, the plants should be pricked out or transplanted, one each into a pint flower-pot filled with rich soil—say one-third well-rotted manure and two-thirds earth—and kept over winter in a cold frame, well protected from frost by linings and coverings, giving air on sunny days.

As soon as the weather is settled, or about the first to the 10th of April, they should be turned out of the pots, without breaking the balls, into the permanent bed; planting them in rows about thirty inches apart, and eighteen inches between the plants. A top dressing of lime or salt, or a mulching of sea-weed, is beneficial to them, as well as to broccoli. They should be well hoed and cared for during their growth, from time to time drawing up some earth around the stems. In dry weather they should have a liberal supply of water, with now and then some manure-water.

When the flower heads show themselves, some of the leaves should be broken over them, in order to protect them from the rain and sun, and to keep the heads close and of a pure white color. They will be fit for use during the month of June or the beginning of July.

Their growth may be accelerated by placing over each plant a small protecting frame, which should be allowed to remain over them until the leaves begin to touch the glass, giving air every fine day. By using a protecting frame, they may be planted out by the beginning of April, or soon after the frost is out of the ground, as they will stand four or five degrees of frost.

Another mode is to transplant the plants, when four or five weeks old, into a cold frame, as in wintering over cabbage plants, and next spring to transplant them with a trowel into the permanent bed. In such a frame they should be pricked out to a distance of six inches apart each way. The soil in the frame should be kept rather dry, for if very damp, and the frames are not kept well aired on sunny, mild days, the plants will be liable to damp off.

Cauliflower seed may also be sown in a hot-bed in January or February, and when the plants are two or three inches high they should be transplanted, two or three inches apart, into boxes or into a spent hot-bed, until the proper time arrives for planting them in the open ground. Such plants, however, do not succeed quite as well as those wintered over.

The best two sorts are the

Early Erfurt; an early, dwarf-growing variety, producing good sized, uniformly close, compact heads.

Early Walcheren; is the same as the broccoli of the same name, and, as before stated, it can hardly be determined whether it is a cauliflower or a broccoli. It is possibly a cross between the two. This succeeds so much better as an autumn crop than any other cauliflower, that we do not recommend any of the true cauliflowers for that purpose. Its cultivation as an autumn crop is found under the head of broccoli.

CELERY.

This is a somewhat troublesome vegetable to grow, as it requires a great deal of management and much labor, especially if the larger sorts are grown in the old method of deep trenches and high banking up. Of late years dwarfer sorts have been introduced, and a less laborious and troublesome method of growing and blanching it has become more general. By some of our later writers on gardening the present method has been claimed to be a new one, but it was in use thirty or more years ago.

It can be grown so as to be fit for the table in August or September, but it is scarcely desirable to do so, as it is seldom wanted at that season of the year, and is not generally as good as that which comes in later in the season. We shall confine ourselves to giving directions for growing the dwarf varieties as a late crop, they being much easier to grow and fully equal for family use to the larger growing sorts.

In the beginning of April, or as soon as the soil will work freely, in an airy spot not exposed to great heat, prepare a seed bed, the soil of which should be well pulverized and enriched with decomposed stable manure, raking it smoothly. Draw drills eight or nine inches apart and half an inch deep, and in them sow the seed rather thinly. After sowing, roll the bed, or with a board press the soil firmly about the seeds. When they are two or three inches high they should be pricked out, four to six inches apart each way, into a nursery-bed of rich earth, in which they may remain for five or six weeks, at which time they will be about seven or eight inches high, and ready to transplant into the regular beds. When pricked out into the nursery bed, they should be watered and lightly shaded for two or three days, and if the weather is dry they should receive frequent and liberal waterings.

The transplanting into the permanent bed may be done at any time in the month of July, or even up to the middle of August. There are many ways of preparing these beds, but we only give directions for two such different modes as involve the least labor.

A bed four to six feet wide, and of any desirable length, should be dug out to a foot in depth, and the soil laid upon the edges of the bed; the bottom is then to be well spaded, and well manured with either short stable or cow manure, or with guano. In this bed the plants are to set in rows fourteen inches apart, and the plants nine inches apart on the rows. When taking them from the nursery bed, be careful to take them up with all their roots attached, and be sure to set them firmly in the soil of the bed. The leaves should be left entire, and not clipped or shortened, only removing any suckers that may grow from the main stem. After planting they should be well watered, and shaded by placing a board about eight or nine inches wide directly over each row, and an inch or two above the plants. The intervening space between the boards will admit light and air; at the end of a week or ten days they will be well established, and the boards can then be removed. During their growth they will be benefited by occasional waterings of weak guano water, being careful not to let it get into the heart of the plant.

From the middle to the end of August, the earthing up process may be begun for such as may be wanted for use in September or October; and about the middle of September for such as may be needed for use in November. When the plants are about fifteen or eighteen inches high, remove any suckers or offshoots, and then take two boards nine inches wide, as long as the width of the bed; place one on each side of a row of plants, close up to them. Then fill in the space between them with the soil taken out of the bed, pulverizing it very finely as it is thrown in, letting it remain as thrown in without treading down. When the spaces between the two rows is filled in to the height of the boards, gently and carefully withdraw them, and do another row in the same way. When the boards are withdrawn, the loose earth will roll down into the spaces between the plants without getting into their hearts, and will make a level earthing up of about six inches. The process is to be repeated two or three times, or every fortnight, according to the height the plants may attain. Some place the boards slightly inclining towards the plants, retaining them in this position by triangular pieces of board shaped like an inverted V. This is done the better to insure the earth falling in between the plants when the boards are removed. Earthing up should be done when the plants are quite dry, for if done when they have dew or rain upon them they will be liable to rust. Thus treated, all the trouble of handling the plants and pressing the soil in between the plants by hand is avoided.

Some gardeners do not commence earthing them up until they have attained nearly their full size, and generally do it at one operation, earthing them as high as can be done without burying their hearts. In this case wider boards will be required. Should the weather continue open and mild, and the plants continue growing, they give them another earthing up about the first of November. Others let the plants make their natural growth, and earth them up at one operation three or four weeks before they are wanted for use. It is not necessary to earth up that which is intended for winter use more than once.

A second mode of growing them is to set out the plants at one foot apart each way, in a level bed of rich soil. Planted thus thickly, the plants retain an erect position but are not as large and strong as when grown by the previous method. The soil between the plants must receive two or three successive hoeings to keep the plants clear of weeds. When grown in this way it is intended for midwinter or later use, being blanched in the preserving pit.

The best mode of preserving it for winter use is to dig out a trench ten or twelve inches wide with square sides, the depth to correspond with the height of the celery, and of any convenient length from four to six or eight feet. Into this trench the celery is placed after it is dug up, just as it comes from the bed, without trimming either the roots or tops. The plants are to be put in upright, one by one, side by side against the sides of the trench, and the earth then filled in. Another trench is then opened alongside the first and about twelve inches from it, and thus one trench after the other until the whole crop is laid in. The tops are to be left uncovered and projecting a couple of inches. The time to commence this operation is about the 20th of October, and it can be continued at intervals of a week apart; that first set in the trench will be fit for use by the first of December, and that last put in can be used until March or April.

When the last lot is put in, the bed should be covered with a layer of small brush to the depth of five or six inches, and on this a layer of leaves, hay or straw should be gradually laid, so that by the middle of December, or when cold weather has steadily set in, it will amount to a foot or more in depth. This mode of covering it with brush, and gradually with other material, will keep it cool and prevent it heating or decaying. As the covering keeps out the frost, the celery can be dug out as wanted during the winter. If there is any danger of water from the surrounding land getting into the bed, an open drain should be opened all around the bed, as the bed should be kept as dry as possible.

The best dwarf sorts are the following:

Early Dwarf Solid White, Incomparable White of some seedsmen, has a solid leaf stalk, compact heart, well flavored, early and hardy, and blanching readily.

Boston Market; is hardy, crisp, solid, mild flavored, not liable to become stringy, and blanches quickly.

Carter's Dwarf Crimson or *Incomparable Dwarf Red* of some, is similar to the *Incomparable White*, but differing from it in color, the leaf stalks being of a rosy crimson color.

CELERIAC.

Is a variety of celery producing roots resembling a turnip or kohl-rabi. The time of sowing the seed and its early culture is the same as celery, but it is grown in level surface beds, and not in trenches, like the celery from the nursery or seed beds. The soil should be well manured, and the plants set out at the same time as celery, in rows eighteen inches apart and six inches between the plants. When planted out, all suckers or side shoots should be removed, and, from time to time, during its growth in the permanent bed, they should be looked over for the same purpose.

Keep the soil well stirred between the plants, and in dry weather water freely, so as to keep them in a constantly growing state. When their growth is nearly completed, they should receive a slight earthing up with the hoe, so as to somewhat blanch the roots, and render them more tender and succulent.

Some persons protect it in winter as directed for celery, others cut the tops off and store them in pits like potatoes, or in boxes of damp sand or earth in a dry cellar. It is a much hardier plant than the common celery.

It is used as a root salad by slicing the roots and serving them with vinegar and oil, by stewing them like turnips and serving them with drawn butter, and slicing and putting them into soups for flavoring purposes. It is a very desirable addition to our list of winter vegetables.

There are three varieties named in the seed catalogues, but the ordinary sort is the best of them.

CHERVIL.

Of this vegetable there are two species, botanically speaking; one grown to be used as parsley for garnishing; the other known as the *Turnip-rooted Chervil*, grown for its roots, which resemble an early horn carrot in size and shape, the flesh being white and mealy, having somewhat the flavor of a sweet potato.

The species grown for its leaves is known as *Curled-leaved Chervil*. The seed should be thinly sown in May, in drills half an inch deep and twelve inches apart. It requires a good rich soil. The leaves are used for garnishing, for putting in salads and for flavoring soups.

The *Turnip-rooted Chervil* is of recent introduction, and is as hardy as the parsnip, its culture being the same. The seeds germinate but slowly in hot, dry weather; they should therefore be sown as early in the spring as the ground is in good working order.

CHICCORY

The leaves of this plant are used as a salad, and the roots as a substitute for, or to adulterate, coffee.

It makes a most excellent winter salad when blanched, and is very easily grown, much resembling endive. The seeds should be sown in May, in drills three-quarters of an inch deep and about fifteen inches apart. The soil should be rich, mellow and well trenched twelve or more inches deep. When the young plants are two or three inches high, they should be thinned out to eight inches apart. The soil should be kept frequently stirred and clear of weeds.

Before being used as a salad the leaves must be blanched, which is done by inverting boxes or flower-pots over them about twelve inches deep, or by placing boards, nailed together at right angles thus ∧, over the rows. When wanted for winter use, the plants are to be taken up late in the fall and planted thickly in a box filled with sand or light earth, and then placed in a cool cellar, watering them after planting. When wanted for use, a box full of them should be placed in a dark room where the temperature will be from 50° to 60°; or they may be placed in the kitchen, and another box, such as a soap box, inverted over them. They will soon start into growth, and afford a supply of blanched leaves for salading purposes. After the leaves are cut off, the roots are of no further use and may be thrown away, bringing another box full to supply their place.

This vegetable is not much used in this country, but is largely used in England, and to a greater extent in Holland and Belgium, as it is so readily grown.

There are five or six varieties grown in Europe; the *Large-rooted*, or *Coffee Chicory*, or the *Magdebourg*, are generally preferred as being the most luxuriant in growth and the most productive.

CHIVES.

This is a well-known species of the onion family. The leaves are the principal parts used, principally for flavoring soups, as an ingredient in spring salads, and for flavoring omelets.

It is very hardy, and will grow in almost any soil. It is propagated by division of the roots, as it seldom, if ever, produces seeds. The bulbs, two or three together, should be set out in May in rows fifteen or eighteen inches apart, the tufts twelve inches apart on the row. To have them young and tender, the plants should be frequently cut down, so as to insure a young growth for use.

COLEWORT.

The true Colewort or Collards is quite distinct from the ordinary cabbage, but is now supposed to be lost to garden cultivation. Its place has been supplied by sowing the seeds of early cabbage in drills a foot apart and half an inch deep, thinning them out to six or eight inches apart, and keeping up a succession by sowings at intervals of two weeks, from the last of April to the last of June, for summer use, and in September for autumn use.

The young plants, when six or eight inches high, are used as spinach.

CORN.

For garden purposes the most suitable sorts to grow are those known as "Sweet." They may be either grown in hills or in rows. When in the former they should be placed three or four feet apart each way. When grown in rows they should be about four feet apart, and the seeds should be planted eight or nine inches apart on the rows. The proper time for planting is from the middle of May until the middle of July, planting at intervals of two weeks, to have a succession of green ears.

Corn requires a light soil, and should be well manured to insure large ears; keep the soil well hoed, and hill up the plants well.

Darling's Early is an early productive variety, of rather dwarf habit, so that the hills may be three feet apart one way and only two and a half feet the other; or the drills may be three feet apart.

Burr's Mammoth is a larger growing, later sort than the preceding. It is a twelve to sixteen rowed variety. It is hardy and productive.

CRESS.

This is an early spring salad, used either alone, or mixed with lettuce and other salad plants to make them piquant.

It should be sown as early in the spring as the ground is in working order. Sow thickly in drills six or eight inches apart, making successive sowings at intervals of a week or ten days apart. Cut it for use when three or four inches high.

There are six or eight varieties, but the curled-leaved is the most useful, as it can be used for garnishing as well as for salads.

CUCUMBER.

Cucumbers require a very rich, warm, moist soil to grow them well.

To forward them and have them early, the seeds should be sown in small flower-pots, one seed in each, from the first to the 15th of April, and then placed in a cool frame, keeping the sashes close and protecting them with coverings if the nights are cool, until the seeds come up, which will be in five or six days. After sowing the seeds they should be watered with milk-warm water, cold water having a tendency to rot them by chilling the soil. After the seeds come up, air should be given every sunny day from nine o'clock in the morning until three or four o'clock in the afternoon, by tilting the sashes or drawing them down three or four inches.

In three or four weeks' time, or when they have two or three rough leaves, the plants will be ready for transplanting out-of-doors, in hills four to six feet apart each way, putting three plants in a hill. Each hill should have one or two shovelfuls of well-rotted manure, well incorporated with the soil. Another mode of forwarding them is to cut sods two or three inches thick and four to six inches square, and placing them, grass side down, side by side in the frame. On each sod place three or four cucumber seeds, and cover them with half an inch of light, rich soil, sifted fine, and watering as before. Their after treatment is the same as that of those started in pots. In transplanting them to the hills, bury the sod about half an inch deeper than the soil with which the seeds were overlaid.

In either mode of starting them, they should be watered and partially shaded for a day or two after being transplanted to the hills. If the weather should be very dry, the hills should occasionally be liberally watered, choosing the evening for doing so.

If protecting boxes can be had, then the seeds may be sown at once in the hills and a box placed over each, treating them the same as to airing and watering as though they were in a frame. By either of these modes the plants will escape being devoured by the striped bug.

Outdoor sowing should be done from the first to the 15th of May, sowing about twenty seeds in a hill and covering them half an inch deep with soil. When such of them as may have escaped the attacks of the bug have developed three or four rough leaves, pull up all but three or four in each hill. Where protectors are used against the ravages of the bug, it will not be necessary to sow more than six or eight seeds in a hill.

Pickling cucumbers in garden culture should be grown in hills six feet apart each way and well manured with decomposed manure. The seed should be sown from the middle of June to the middle of July, seeding liberally as before, to make up for the ravages of the bug. As soon as the cucumbers are of suitable size for pickling, the beds should be gone over every day or two to gather them, as when left to grow large the plants are not so productive.

There are numerous varieties of the cucumber, but the following are the best for family use:

White-spined; it grows from six to eight inches long, is of good flavor, crisp and tender. It is very productive and does not soon turn yellow; it is also a good variety for pickling when very small pickles are not wanted.

Long Green Turkey. This variety grows from fifteen to eighteen inches long. It is slender and has but few seeds, and is very well suited for serving on the table unsliced. It is very productive, of excellent flavor, crisp and firm. On account of its having but few seeds, it is an excellent sort for large pickles.

Short Green or Gherkin; is mostly used for pickling; it is hardy, productive and well flavored. There is a sort known as *Underwood's Short Prickly,* which is said to be an improvement upon the original variety in being more crisp and solid.

DANDELION.

This plant, now so common in our fields and gardens, was originally introduced from Europe, and in its indigenous state in this country is an escape from our gardens.

When cultivated in good rich garden soil it makes admirable spring greens, and when blanched, a salad resembling endive. The seed should be sown in May or June, in good rich deep soil. Sow in drills half an inch deep, and twelve or fifteen inches apart, and in July thin out the plants to three or four inches apart. The following spring they will be fit for use. When wanted as a salad, blanch the heads as directed for endive.

As it is an early as well as a most healthful vegetable, it is again coming into use.

EGG PLANT.

The seeds of this plant require a considerable amount of heat to cause them to vegetate freely—hence they should be sown in a hot-bed about the end of March or the beginning of April, keeping the sashes on and covering them at night until the young plants show themselves; then a little air may be given in the middle of the day if bright and warm. If a hot-bed cannot be had, some seeds may be sown in flower-pots, and started on the inside sill of a sunny window of the kitchen or other warm room.

When the plants are two or three inches high, they should be pricked out into small pots, one plant in each, replaced in the frame, and watered and shaded for three or four days, until they make new roots. About the first week in June they may be turned out of the pots and planted in the open ground, in a warm sheltered border, at a distance of two and a half to three feet apart each way. The soil cannot be made too rich for them. When they are about a foot high, draw the earth up to them, as in hilling any other vegetables.

One or two dozen plants will produce enough of fruit for a small family.

The best two sorts are the *New York Improved* and the *Black Pekin*. The first is distinguished from the other purple varieties, in being more stocky and robust in growth, and in having the stems and leaves thickly set with spines. It is also more productive than the others.

The *Black Pekin* has very dark purple, almost black fruit, of a globular shape, large and very solid. It is somewhat earlier than the first named sort and very productive.

The white, striped and scarlet varieties are not worth cultivating in the kitchen garden, being only serviceable as ornamental plants.

ENDIVE.

Endive, like lettuce, is a salad plant that can be had all through the summer and autumn; but as the early sown crop is liable to run to seed, owing to the heat of our summers, it is generally grown as an autumn salad.

There are two distinct classes of it cultivated, of each of which there are also several varieties. The one is known as *Curl-leaved Endive* by the English, and by the French is called *Chicoree des Jardins*, and, with its varieties, has curled or frizzled leaves. The other class, with its varieties, is known as *Batavian Endive* by the English, and by the French is called *Scarolle*. It has broad smooth leaves.

If early crops should be desired, the seed may be sown at the same time as early lettuce, and the plants set out and cultivated in the same way. They require the same kind of soil as lettuce. For the autumn crop the seed should be sown in June or July, and when the plants are three or four inches high, which will be in August or September, they should be planted out in rows one foot apart each away. The Batavian sorts, having larger leaves than the curled-leaved sorts, will require to be planted fifteen inches apart each way. If the planting is not done in cloudy or moist weather, they should be watered when planted. The after cultivation is the same as lettuce.

It is always blanched before it is used, as otherwise it has a bitter, unpleasant taste. There are three or four ways of doing this. When the root leaves of the plants have attained their full size, the leaves are to be gathered up, and tied together at their tips with a bit of twine or bast matting. The outer leaves thus tied up exclude the air and light, and thus blanch the interior leaves. They should be tied up when quite dry, for if wet the interior leaves will decay.

Another mode is to invert a flower-pot over each plant, closing the hole in the bottom. A still better way is to lay a piece of flat board, ten or twelve inches square, over each plant; or a plank or board of that width can be laid over as many plants on the row as its length will cover. As the crop is not all needed at once, only as many plants as are likely to be needed for three or four days' use should be blanched at one time. If the weather is warm, they will blanch in ten or twelve days, but as the season gets cooler it will require three or four weeks to finish the process.

When wanted for winter use, tie up the leaves as before directed, before frost sets in, and then take up the plants carefully, with a ball of earth to each, and set them out in boxes filled with light earth in a light warm cellar, watering them after planting, but being careful not to put any water on the leaves. They should be taken up when dry, all dead or decayed leaves removed, and the plants not allowed to touch each other in the boxes. In this way they may be kept until spring.

The French and Germans have several sorts of endive, but with us the *Green-curled* among the *Chicoree* sorts, and the small Batavian among the *Scarolles*, are the two best, both bleaching readily, and not being as bitter as some other varieties.

FETTICUS.

This vegetable is chiefly grown as a winter and early spring salad, although it is sometimes used boiled as greens or spinach.

It requires a rich soil. The seed may be sown towards the end of August or the beginning of September in drills six or eight inches apart and half an inch deep, rolling them after sowing. When the plants are well up, thin them out to three or four inches apart. Keep it well hoed and clear of weeds, and when severe weather sets in, give it a slight covering of straw or salt hay, as is done with spinach, removing it in March or April.

It can also be sown early in the spring, as soon as the ground is in working order, and will be ready for use in six or eight weeks afterwards.

GARLIC.

The root of this plant is composed of numerous small bulbs, called "cloves" or "sets." It requires a light, rich soil. The cloves should be planted in April or May an inch deep, in rows twelve inches apart, and five or six inches apart on the rows. The soil should be kept loose and clear of weeds, and when the tops wither, which will be some time in August, the bulbs will be fit to gather. They should be kept the same as onions.

GARDEN PATIENCE.

This plant, which is a species of dock, is seldom if ever grown as a vegetable in this country, but is used in the place of spinach in some parts of Europe, especially in Sweden, where they cut and boil the young, tender leaves, adding about a fourth part of sorrel to them, making an excellent dish.

It is a hardy perennial, growing four to five feet high, and will grow in almost any soil. The seeds should be sown in April or May, in drills fifteen inches apart and an inch deep, and when the plants are three or four inches high they should be thinned out to ten or twelve inches apart. To make it produce large-sized leaves abundantly, the flower stems should be cut out as soon as they develop themselves. It may be cut for three or four years.

The common *Yellow Dock*, which is a somewhat troublesome weed, when treated in the same way also yields a very wholesome substitute for spinach or greens.

HORSE-RADISH.

As the long, tapering roots of this vegetable are the parts used, it is necessary, in order to have them in perfection, to follow such a course of cultivation as will most fully develop them. To this end it is necessary that the soil should be deep, rich and mellow. In a dry, gravelly soil, or a soil that has a hard, clayey subsoil, it does not do well.

The old practice was to plant the crown of the roots in the spring or autumn in a deeply-trenched soil, and cultivate it two years before taking the crop. When grown from the crowns they fork off into several small roots, which cannot in a single season attain a proper size for use, and are liable to be hollow and otherwise imperfect. The modern mode of growing it is as follows:

Early in the spring prepare a bed of any size deemed necessary, by trenching a piece of rich soil two feet deep, laying a good dressing of manure in the bottom of each trench, digging it lightly into the bottom soil, but not mixing it with the soil above, as this induces the growth of numerous fibrous side roots. Line the bed out in rows two feet apart, and plant root sets sixteen or eighteen inches apart on the row. These sets should be sound, solid pieces of the roots from three-eighths to half an inch in diameter, cut from four to six inches long. With a dibble of suitable diameter make holes at the distances indicated above; into each of these holes drop a set, being very careful to have the top end uppermost in the hole, the depth of which should be so proportioned to the length of the set as to permit the top end to be covered with soil not over an inch in depth. Press the soil closely and firmly to the set. The after cultivation simply consists in keeping it clear of weeds.

In the months of November or December the roots will be ready for use, and should then be dug up, the leaves removed, and the roots packed away in boxes of moist earth in a cellar, or kept with other vegetables in a preserving pit.

If a large supply is not wanted, a trench two feet wide and two feet deep, of any desired length, may be opened in any convenient part of the garden, well manured at the bottom, and planted along the centre with a single row of sets.

JERUSALEM ARTICHOKE.

This plant is misnamed, as it is not an artichoke, but a species of sunflower with tuberous roots, which are the parts used for culinary purposes. Before the introduction of the potato it was in common use, but is now but seldom cultivated.

It requires the same kind of cultivation as the potato, and is propagated by cutting the tubers into sets with two eyes to each, keeping the ground loose by frequent hoeings. It is perfectly hardy, and in removing the crop, care should be had to gather all the tubers, for if left in the ground, they will start into growth the succeeding spring and become troublesome weeds.

There are three or four varieties, differing mainly in the color of the skin of the tubers.

KOHL-RABI, OR TURNIP-ROOTED CABBAGE.

This vegetable belongs to the cabbage tribe, but the stem swells out, assuming a globular form resembling a turnip, this being the edible part.

It requires the same soil and treatment as the turnip, and as it does not bear transplanting well, it should always be raised from seeds sown in the bed where it is to be grown. The soil should be rich and mellow, so as to induce a rapid, quick growth, and so produce a tender, succulent bulb stalk, for such it really is, being simply an adpressed, enlarged cabbage stem.

The seed should be sown in this section during the month of June, but may be sown in May or July, according to latitude. It should be sown in rows eighteen inches apart, and after the plants have come up, they should be thinned out to ten or twelve inches apart. The after cultivation consists in keeping the beds well hoed and clear of weeds. The proper time for using the bulbs is when they are three or four inches in diameter.

There are seven or eight varieties grown, but the best for garden purposes is the *Early White Vienna*. Of this there is a purple variety, but it only differs from the first in color.

LEEK

The soil for this vegetable can scarcely be made too rich and mellow, or kept too mellow.

The seed should be sown in a seed bed in good rich soil, in a sheltered situation, towards the end of March or early in April, in drills an inch deep and eight to ten inches apart. The beds should be kept scrupulously clean of weeds and well worked. In June or July they should be transplanted into the permanent bed, the rows being one foot apart, and the plants six inches apart on the rows. This bed should be well spaded to a depth of ten or twelve inches. Great care should be taken not to injure the roots, and the plants should be set with a large blunt dibble, or in an open trench with a spade. After the plants have taken root, the beds should be kept well hoed and free from weeds.

If the leeks are wanted in a blanched state, they may be planted in trenches four inches deep, and the earth gradually drawn into the trench as the plants progress in growth.

In this section they are generally dug up in November, planted in trenches, and protected as celery is.

There are eight or ten varieties in the seed catalogues, but the sorts most generally grown are the *London Flag* and the *Musselburgh*, preferably the latter. The *Large Rouen* is a favorite French sort that attains a great size.

LETTUCE.

The numerous varieties of lettuce may be divided into two classes—those that are hardy, or comparatively so, suitable for winter use, and those that are tender, and only suitable for summer use.

The hardy sorts may be sown from the first to the middle of September in an open border of rich soil, sowing thinly in drills six inches apart and one-quarter of an inch deep. In about a month or six weeks they will be large enough to transplant into a cold frame, putting them about two inches apart each way. When cold weather sets in, the sashes are to be put on the frames, and during the winter all the attention they will require is to give them plenty of air on bright days, with a light covering of straw, old carpet or matting when the weather is very severe—as, when the thermometer indicates twelve or fifteen degrees of frost. They are as hardy as cabbage plants, but if not kept well aired, they become more susceptible to the cold and are less robust.

In the month of March, or as soon as the ground is in working order, these plants may be transplanted into a good rich warm border, and will be fit to cut for use in May. They should be planted in rows, twelve inches apart each way.

As early cabbages are planted at the same time, it is the custom of some of our market gardeners to set them two feet apart on the row, and set a lettuce plant midway between each, which becomes fit to use long before the cabbage grows large enough to interfere with it; by this means much room and some labor is saved.

Another mode is to sow the seed very thinly in a dry, warm, sheltered bed, leaving it out all winter, but protecting it with leaves or a sprinkling of straw when frost sets in. Some persons sow a sprinkling of seed along with autumn-sown spinach, but it repays the trouble to transplant them into frames, as above directed.

The tender or summer lettuce should be sown in a cold frame in February or March, being careful to keep the frame well covered up at night, but airing it well during the day, to prevent the plants being drawn up. These plants will be ready to set out in April or May, or when they are about two inches high.

The soil for lettuce can scarcely be too rich, for to have it in its greatest perfection it must be grown rapidly. The soil should be well hoed every two weeks after planting, as lettuce thrives best in soil that is frequently stirred and kept open.

Lettuce can be forwarded or had very early in the season by setting out the young plants in February or March, seven or eight inches apart, in a cold frame, the soil having two or three inches deep of rotted manure dug into it. The frame should be well covered up at night, and air given during the middle of the day, increasing the airing as the season progresses. Care must be had to water them frequently with tepid water, so that they may be kept in a constantly growing state.

When wanted very early, in the form of leaf lettuce, it may be sown rather thickly broadcast in a hot-bed in February. When the leaves are from three to four inches high it will be fit to cut.

The best hardy sorts for winter frames, are the

Early Simpson; a variety of the curled Silesia. It does not form a close, compact head, but is very tender, of excellent quality, and very early.

Tennis Ball; this variety forms a close, hard head of rather small size. It is very hardy, and slow in going to seed.

Hammersmith Hardy; this is the hardiest sort cultivated. The leaves are very succulent, the heads small. It soon runs to seed in warm weather.

Green Winter Cabbage is also a very hardy sort, does not run to seed readily, and forms a firm, solid, medium-sized head.

For summer use the best are the *Large India;* it has a very large, somewhat loose head, is very crisp and tender, and withstands heat and dry weather admirably.

Neapolitan has a very large, round, hard, close head, and is very slow in running to seed.

There is a class of lettuces known as *Coss Lettuces,* which have long, straight leaves, that require to be tied up over the head to blanch it. They are much esteemed in Europe, but in our own climate quickly run to seed. They should therefore be set out very early in the season, but are not sufficiently hardy to winter over. Of the many varieties grown abroad, the *Paris Green Coss* does the best in this climate.

MARTYNIA.

The long, horn-shaped seed-pods of this plant are used for pickling when in their young, green state, and by many persons are preferred to cucumbers. The seed should be sown in an open border in April or May, and in June should be transplanted into the permanent bed at a distance of two or two and a half feet apart each way.

It will thrive in any good garden soil, but does not need to be heavily manured.

MELONS.

The cultivation of the melon is in all respects the same as that of the cucumber, only that they should not be planted less than six feet apart each way. If the growth is very luxuriant, the ends of the leading shoots should be pinched off, in order to check the growth and make the fruit set better. The fruit also should be thinned out if too many set—it increases the size and flavor; and four or five fruits to a plant are as many as should be allowed to remain. When the fruit becomes as large as a goose egg, it is well to put a shingle, a slate or some similar material under each, as it somewhat hastens their maturity, and renders them better flavored. An occasional watering of guano water has a tendency to increase the size of the fruit.

Of the two classes of melons—namely, the yellow-fleshed or Cantaloupes, and the green-fleshed or Musk Melons—we consider the latter as the only class worth cultivating in this country. The varieties are very numerous, but the following two are fully equal to any of the others.

Skillman's Netted is of comparatively small size; it is early, very sugary, melting and high flavored; it is also a compact grower.

Green Citron is of large size, very sugary, juicy, and of delicious flavor. It bears abundantly and is comparatively hardy.

MUSHROOMS.

The cultivation of this delicious esculent is not often attempted by amateur gardeners. The old system of cultivation involved a great deal of trouble, and had not a little of a certain kind of mystery, but of late years the French, who grow large quantities of them, have greatly simplified the process. One of their modes is the following, by which any person having a warm, dry cellar, and a supply of fresh horse manure, can obtain a liberal supply:

In an open shed, or in any place protected from heavy rains, ordinary fresh horse manure, free from rubbish or long straw, is to be laid up in beds of two or more feet thick, pressing it down with the fork as it is laid up, and when finished treading it down firmly with the feet. It should then be thoroughly watered and again trodden down, and left to ferment for eight or ten days. At the expiration of this time it must be turned over with the fork and made again into a similar bed, care being taken that the outsides of the previous bed should form the centre of the new bed. In another ten days or a fortnight it will be ready for use. Tubs are then to be provided, which may be done by sawing flour barrels in halves crosswise, and boring four or five half inch holes in the bottom of each for drainage. Fill the tubs two or three inches deep with any good fresh garden soil, and add the prepared manure until the tub is half full. Place six or seven pieces of spawn, each about the size of a hen's egg, upon the manure in each tub, and fill the tub full of manure, pressing it well down and rounding off the top dome-shaped. The spawn, which may be obtained of any of our seedsmen, comes in the shape and size of common bricks. At the end of ten days, if the spawn have taken—which may be known by its developing white, thread-like filaments—cover it with an inch or two of fresh soil screened through a coarse sieve.

The tubs, when made up, should be placed in a dark cellar, free from draughts of cold air, in which the temperature can be kept as nearly as possible at 50 degrees. The main points to be attended to are that the temperature of the manure is at its proper height (about 76 degrees Fahr.) when the spawn is inserted, and that it should not be covered with soil until the spawn is well developed. Should the soil and manure in the tubs become dry, they should be watered by sprinkling them with water at about blood-heat or 100 degrees.

In a few days the mushrooms will show themselves. They should be gathered every other day, by breaking off in the soil—a slight twist with the hand facilitating this operation. Never use a knife to gather them, and fill up with fresh soil any hole that may be made in pulling them. They will continue yielding for three or four weeks; and a second but smaller crop can be obtained after the first is gathered, by giving another dressing of fresh soil about half an inch thick, beating it down moderately with the spade and watering it with blood-warm water.

MUSTARD.

Of the two species of cultivated mustard, the white is that generally grown for garden purposes. The young plants, when about three inches high, are used as a salad, like cress, on account of their piquancy, and the seeds are used in pickles, to which they impart a pungent, pleasant flavor.

When grown for salading purposes, the seeds should be thickly sown in the open ground as early in the spring as the season will permit, in drills six inches apart and half an inch deep. If wanted earlier they may be sown in a frame. A succession may be kept up by sowing every week or ten days.

When grown for the seeds, sow early in the spring, in rows about fifteen inches apart. The seed should be quite thinly sown, so that the plants will not choke each other; the new crop will be ready to gather by August.

Any good garden soil will suit it.

NASTURTIUM.

The unripe succulent seed-pods of this well-known plant are used for pickling, being an excellent substitute for capers. Any good garden soil suits it; if it is comparatively poor it will be for the better, as the plant has a tendency to run to growth at the expense of flowering and fruiting freely.

The seeds should be sown in May, in drills three feet apart, and about six inches apart on the row. The plants should have pea-brush set to them when they are about six inches high, on which they may climb. This preserves the green seed-pods from the sand or soil, and from rotting.

The pods should be gathered when of the size of a small pea; if left on the plant too long the seed within them becomes hardened, which renders them unfit for use. Sometimes the young shoots are used as a salad alone, or for mixing with lettuce.

The best variety for kitchen garden purposes is the common *Dwarf*.

NEW ZEALAND SPINACH.

This is not really a spinach, but its leaves are used in the same way. It is very useful for this purpose, as it grows freely, and flourishes under the heat of our summer's sun.

It requires a rich, moist, well-pulverized soil. The seeds may be sown in the open ground from April to July, in drills three feet apart and two inches deep. The plants should be about a foot apart on the row. In five or six weeks after sowing the gathering of the leaves for use may be commenced, taking care not to injure the ends of the young shoots. The gathering may be continued until frost, as the leaves retain their succulence through the summer.

If the weather should be very dry, give the plants plenty of water.

Fifteen or twenty plants will supply a large family.

OKRA.

The unripe seed-pods of this plant, known in the South as Gumbo, are used sliced up to thicken soups and similar dishes, to which they also impart a rich flavor.

It thrives in any good garden soil. The seed should be sown in May, in drills an inch deep and two feet apart, two or three seeds being dropped together every foot of distance on the row. After the plants have grown beyond the seed leaf, thin them out to single plants. Earth them up slightly two or three times during their growth.

The *Dwarf* variety, growing from two to two and a half feet high, is best adapted for our northern climate; the *Tall* or *Giant* sort, growing five or six feet high, taking up too much room in our gardens.

The pods, transversely sliced and dried when green, may be kept for winter use.

ONION.

Onions require a rich, finely-pulverized soil, in order to grow them to perfection. The ground should be prepared as early in the spring as possible, by heavily manuring it with well-rotted manure, digging and pulverizing the soil as finely as possible. Composted poultry manure, fine ground bone-dust or soot, sown in the drills and then covered with an inch or two of soil, are excellent manures for this vegetable. A top dressing of wood ashes after the plants are well up also assists their growth materially.

The seed should be sown from the first to the 15th of April, in drills one inch deep and one foot apart; a light roller should be run along each drill as soon as the seed is covered in. When the plants are well up, the ground should be well hoed, and the plants thinned out to two or three inches apart. The hoeing should be repeated two or three times, but discontinued after the bulbs begin to set, as it is then injurious to them. If weeds should then make their appearance, they must be removed by hand.

When the tops wither, which is generally in August, the bulbs should be pulled up and left on the ground exposed to the sun and air for two or three weeks, in order to well dry them off; after which they must be kept in a cool, dry cellar, but free from frost.

If it is desired to have green onions very early in the spring, the seed should be sown in August or early in September, and the young onions protected on the approach of cold weather by having some long litter thrown over them along the rows.

Another mode of raising them is from sets. These are raised by sowing the seed, in April, very thickly, in drills nine inches apart, in a piece of poor or unmanured soil, for if the bulbs get any larger than a hazel nut they will be very apt to run to seed when planted out for the main crop. In August, when ripe, they should be taken up and well dried, after which they should be placed, with their chaff skins on, on the floor of a garret or hay-loft, covering them, when cold weather sets in, with six or eight inches of hay or straw. They will keep, thus protected, until spring. In April of the ensuing spring they are to be planted in a piece of very rich soil in rows twelve inches apart; a bulb being pressed into the ground with the thumb and forefinger every three inches on the row, and then rolled with a light roller to set them still more firmly. The beds should be kept clean between the rows by occasional hoeing; but all weeds growing between the bulbs, or within three or four inches of them on the rows, should be removed by hand.

The sets from top onions are treated in the same way. They are raised by planting the full grown bulbs, in the spring, in rows fifteen inches apart, and the bulbs ten inches apart. During the summer they will throw up stems, producing a cluster of ten or twelve small bulbs, instead of a head of flowers and seeds. These sets are to be preserved over winter in the same way as sets raised from seeds, and planted and treated the ensuing season in the same way.

The potato onion increases by division of the root. Small bulbs are generally planted early in the spring in rich soil, in rows a foot apart, the bulbs being set six inches apart on the row. They should be inserted just deep enough in the soil to cover the crown, and should be firmly set in the ground. As they grow, they split up or divide into six or eight good-sized bulbs. They may be planted in September, and on the approach of winter covered with a slight covering of long manure, litter or leaves, removing the covering as soon as spring commences. They give a larger crop when planted in the autumn than when planted in the spring.

There are numerous varieties of the onion; but the selection of sorts for our climate may be restricted to three, excluding top and potato onions.

The *Wethersfield Large Red* is very productive and an excellent keeper, but strong flavored.

The *Yellow Onion*, misnamed the *Silver Skinned* in New England, is much milder and sweeter flavored than the *Large Red*. It is very productive and a good keeper. There is a sub-variety of this, known as the *Danvers Yellow*; it is exceedingly productive, but is not as good a keeper.

The *White Portugal*, or *Silver Skinned*, has a pure white skin, with the upper part of the bulb veined with green. It is very mild flavored and productive, but is not a good keeper, unless the bulbs are exposed to light in a dry, airy place free from frost. It is largely used for pickling, for this purpose being grown as directed for sowing sets, only not sowing the seed over half an inch deep; this prevents the bulbs having thick necks, and makes them more solid and compact.

Of the top onion there are two varieties, the red and the

white. The flesh is coarser than the seed-bearing sorts, and the bulbs are not as good keepers, unless kept very dry and cool.

There is but one variety of the top onion. It is mild, sweet flavored and of excellent quality. To facilitate its keeping well, two or three inches of the stem should be left on each bulb.

Where, owing to the effects of climate or the persistent attacks of insects, onions cannot be successfully raised from seed, recourse must be had to sets—especially the potato onion.

ORACHE, OR FRENCH SPINACH.

This vegetable requires a rich, deep, moist soil. The leaves and tender stalks have a pleasant, slightly acid taste, and are cooked and used in the same manner as spinach. The cultivation is also the same. There are several varieties, varying chiefly in the color of the leaves, which, however, all turn green when boiled. Unless used when young and tender, the leaves are apt to be tough and stringy.

PARSLEY.

Parsley requires a rich mellow soil to grow it in perfection, and as the seed vegetates slowly, especially in hot, dry weather, it is important to sow it as early as possible in April. The soil should be deep and finely pulverized, and the seed sown in drills a foot apart, and from half an inch to an inch in depth. It is a good practice to sow a light sprinkling of radish seed with it, as it vegetates quickly, thus marking out the rows to facilitate weeding and keeping the ground open.

After the plants are about three inches high, thin them out to six or eight inches apart, and keep them clean by frequent hoeings.

To have it for winter use, cut off all the old leaves in the month of September; the plants will then make a new growth of leaves. Some of these roots should be taken up early in November, and planted in a cold frame or in boxes to be placed in a light dry cellar; the remainder may be left in the rows, out-of-doors, protecting the plants with a light sprinkling of straw. Thus treated they will be fit for use in the spring before the new sowings are ready to use.

Some gardeners sow the seed in a cold frame in April, between the rows of early lettuce, and let it remain there during the succeeding summer and winter, cutting it off, as before, early in September. This method saves the trouble of transplanting it.

The best sort for general use is the *Dwarf Curled*. When quantities are used for garnishing, and something very elegant is desired for this purpose, the *Moss* or *Fimbriated-leaved* may be sown.

Another variety of parsley, with large fleshy roots, known as the *Hamburgh* or *Turnip-rooted Parsley*, is grown for the sake of its roots, which are used in soups, or as a separate dish, like carrots or parsnips. The seed should be sown in April or May in deep mellow soil, but not too rich, in rows fourteen or fifteen inches apart, thinning out the plants to six or eight inches apart, and treating them afterwards as carrots or parsnips. The roots should be taken up in October, packed in sand or dry earth, and stored in a dry cellar for winter use.

Still another variety, the *Naples Parsley*, is grown for the same uses as celery. The seeds may be sown in a hotbed in March, or in a seed bed in the open air in May.

When the plants are four or five inches high they should be transplanted into good rich soil, in trenches two feet apart and six or eight inches deep, setting the plants a foot apart. As the plants grow the trenches are to be gradually filled in to blanch it. To preserve it for winter use, treat it the same as directed for celery.

PARSNIP.

The parsnip requires a deep, rich soil, and preferably one that has been manured the previous autumn. The seeds can be sown from the middle of March to the middle of May; but as the roots require a long season to enable them to grow to a good size, the earlier the seed is sown, the better.

The drills should be about an inch deep and fourteen to fifteen inches apart, sowing the seeds quite thickly. When grown as a field crop, the rows should be twenty inches apart, so that they can be readily worked with a cultivator or horse hoe. When the plants are about three inches high, they should be thinned out to six or eight inches apart. The after culture consists in keeping them entirely free from weeds by frequent hoeings.

As the parsnip is quite hardy, such portion of the crop as may not be wanted for winter use may be left out in the ground all winter. Those that are wanted for winter use should be taken up late in the autumn, and stored away in the same manner as carrots or turnips. As the roots descend to a great depth into the soil, great care is necessary in taking them up, for if the roots are broken off where they are of any thickness, they will lose much of their flavor and sweetness.

The sorts generally grown are the *Dutch*, the *Guernsey*

and the *Hollow-crowned*; they are very closely alike, and appear to owe what little distinction there may be between them to the differences of soil in which they may be grown. The *Hollow-crowned* appears to have a somewhat shorter and stouter root than the others, and perhaps is to be preferred on that account. Another variety, called the *Student*, is considered to be sweeter and milder flavored than the others.

PEAS.

Peas do best in light, warm soil, but will grow well in heavier soils if they are well drained. Well-rotted horse manure or fine bone-dust suits them best. It is preferable to apply the horse manure the autumn previous. Guano is also an excellent manure for them, when sown in the drills at the rate of a pint to twenty feet of row, stirring it well into the soil for a couple of inches in the bottom of the drill.

The sowing of peas may be commenced in March, or as soon as the ground is in working order. If only one or two sorts are grown, a succession can be had by making sowings at intervals of twelve or fourteen days. But if several sorts, varying in their time of maturity, are sown at the same time, a regular succession can be had in that way. There are various ways of growing them—as in ridges, drills, single or double rows, and with or without sticks or brush. For private gardens, double rows in drills are generally adopted in this country, using or not using sticks, according to the character of the variety sown.

The double rows should be from eighteen inches to four feet apart, according to the height of the variety, the general rule being to make the distances equal to the height to which it grows. The two drills composing the double row should be eight or nine inches apart, and about three inches deep, the peas being sown from half an inch to an inch apart on the row; the early, small-seeded varieties being sown closer than the larger-seeded, tall-growing varieties. Some of the English growers sow them in long single rows, twenty or more feet apart, and not in a succession of rows, as they find that the outside rows, when planted in the ordinary way, always bear more profusely than the inside rows. They also stop or pinch off the leading shoots when the plants are about half the height to which they usually attain, repeating the operation for two or three times after the shoot has made three joints of growth. This renders the plants more stocky, and makes them produce much larger crops, but also has the effect of retarding the crop, as the plants do not set their pods freely until the stopping ceases.

When the plants are from four to six inches high, they should be earthed up, drawing the earth up lightly on each side, in such a way as to have the plants standing in a slight channel along the ridge. When the varieties grown are such as to require staking, this operation should be done before the plants have grown tall enough to fall over. The brush stake should be set along the middle of the ridge between the two rows of plants, and outside of them on each side a shorter row of brush. Where brush is not easily obtained, stakes may be driven in, five or six feet apart, and lines of twine of any kind, six inches apart, may be fastened to the stakes; but brush is the best when it can be had.

If the weather is very hot and dry, mildew is apt to attack the plants and destroy the crop. To destroy the mildew, dredging the foliage with flour of sulphur is the best remedy. To prevent it, water the rows copiously with water, preferably that in which guano has been dissolved in the proportion of three half pints to twenty-five gallons of water.

The varieties of peas are very numerous, new sorts being originated and introduced every year; few of them, however, hold their place in the catalogues for many years. They may be divided into two classes—the smooth-seeded, and the wrinkled. The first comprise as yet the earliest varieties; but none of them are as large, sweet and high flavored as the wrinkled sorts. Other things being equal, the smooth-seeded are scarcely worth growing, when the wrinkled sorts can be had. At present, of the sorts most highly recommended in the catalogues, the following sorts may be selected as the best early varieties:

Carter's First Crop; a very early and productive variety, growing two and a half feet high. A smooth pea.

Daniel O'Rourke; very early and productive; grows three feet high, and is the sort generally grown for the early New York market. Also a smooth pea.

Laxton's Alpha; an extra early variety of its kind. It is a blue, wrinkled marrow pea, very productive, and of excellent quality. Grows three feet high.

McLean's Little Gem; is an early, dwarf, green, wrinkled marrow pea, growing only a foot high. It is very productive and of excellent flavor.

McLean's Blue Peter; is also an early, blue, wrinkled pea, prolific, of fine flavor, and growing a foot high.

McLean's Advance; is a wrinkled pea growing about two feet high. It is nearly as early as the *O'Rourke,* and rich flavored.

Later varieties:

Champion of England; one of the best and most popular of the wrinkled peas, being largely grown for the New

York market. It is very productive and high flavored; growing five feet high.

Veitch's Perfection; is a rich flavored marrow pea, very productive, and one of the best for main or late crops. Height, four feet.

Blue Imperial; an old variety of good flavor and yields abundantly. It is very hardy and thrives in almost any soil; it also withstands the heat better than any other variety. Height, three feet.

PEPPERS OR CAPSICUMS.

These are generally grown in our gardens for the purpose of pickling in their green or half ripe state.

A light sandy soil suits them best, but fair crops can be obtained upon almost any soil, if it is well manured and kept well stirred with the hoe. The seeds may be sown in drills half an inch deep and six inches apart, in a hot-bed, about the first week in April, or in pots or boxes in a kitchen window, as directed for egg-plants; or they may be sown in a warm border early in May. When the plants are two inches high, they should be planted out in rows two feet apart, and from fifteen to eighteen inches apart on the row. If the fruit is not wanted early in the season, the seed may be sown in the open ground where they are to remain, towards the end of May, in drills two feet apart and half an inch deep, dropping three or four seeds at the distance apart the plants are to stand, and when they are an inch or two high pulling up all but one plant.

The after culture consists in deep hoeings of the ground and keeping it clear of weeds.

There are five or six sorts generally grown.

The *Bell* or *Bull Nose* is a large, early, sweet and pleasant flavored variety, with less pungency than some of the other sorts. It can readily be grown by sowing the seeds in the open ground in May. A sort known in the seed catalogues as the *Sweet Mountain* appears to be identical with this.

Cherry Pepper is a small, round-fruited, very pungent variety. It requires to be raised in a hot-bed. There is also a yellow-fruited variety of this sort.

Long Red is a long-fruited sort, frequently used pulverized, as a substitute for the cayenne pepper of commerce. It should be raised in a hot-bed. There is also a yellow-fruited variety of this sort.

Squash Pepper; this sort is largely grown for market purposes, being of large size, and, when correct to name, very thick-fleshed. It is rather more pungent than the *Bell* or the *Sweet Spanish.* It can be grown by sowing the seed in the open air in May.

Sweet Spanish is a large-fruited sort, and very early. It is sweet, mild and pleasant flavored, with scarcely any pungency, and on that account is preferred by many persons. It succeeds well sown in the open ground in May.

PHYTOLACCA.

This is well known throughout the country as "Garget," "Poke-berry" and "Pigeon-berry," and is a common weed by road-sides, waste places and on newly burned pine-lands. It is, however, an excellent substitute for asparagus, which it resembles in taste. The young shoots, as they appear in the spring, before the leaves develop, are the parts used.

The size and quality of the shoots are much improved

by cultivation, especially if they are blanched in the same way as is directed for sea-kale.

The berries and roots are reputed to have medicinal if not poisonous qualities, but the young shoots are not so.

It should be grown in rich deep soil, the plants being set about twelve or fifteen inches apart.

POTATO.

The potato delights in a dry, light, loamy soil, preferably a fresh pasture land with the sod turned under the autumn previous to planting. In stiff, clayey soils, especially if they have been long under cultivation, they are very liable to disease, to be of inferior quality and lacking in productiveness.

In fresh lands they do not require much manure, and in any soils dry or absorbent manures are the best. Such as fine ground bone, superphosphate of lime, ashes, horn shavings and comb-makers' waste. When these cannot be had, well-rotted manure, sea-weed or decayed leaves may be used. Fresh, strong, stimulating manures should always be avoided; but whatever manure is used, it should be spread evenly over the ground, and well plowed in, and not put into the drills or hills, as is generally the practice. Whatever manure is used, it is best to apply it to the soil and plow it in the autumn previous to planting.

There has been much discussion as to whether it is best to plant cut sets or small whole tubers, but good crops have been and can be raised by either method, provided always that the sets are cut from well ripened potatoes, or that the small tubers are well ripened. This cannot be too much insisted upon; if, in either case, they are not thoroughly ripened, the crop will be reduced in yield and very liable to disease. Do not, from a mistaken economy, reserve for sale or table use the largest and best potatoes and save the poorest for planting; if you do, the future crop will certainly be inferior both in quality and quantity; but, on the contrary, save the best for your next season's planting.

When sets are used, cut or divide the potato so that two eyes shall be on each set, and spread them out on a floor, not exposed to the direct rays of the sun, to dry, for three or four days or a week.

For the very early crop, the sets or tubers may be planted as early in April as the ground is in a dry, friable state; the succession and main crops may be planted at any time up to the middle of June. For garden purposes, drills are preferable to hills; the drills being from two and a half to three feet apart, and in dry, light soils five or six inches deep. In very heavy or wet soils they should only be half this depth. Some cultivators having such soils plant the sets on the surface and draw the earth over them. The sets should be planted from eight to ten inches apart on the row. As soon as the plants come up the soil should be hoed, and as the plants continue to grow, up to the time of their coming into flower, they should receive two or three earthings up, so as to cause them to make plenty of side roots, as on the extremities of these the tubers are formed. After they commence to bloom, no further cultivation is necessary, except to pull up any tall weeds that may show themselves.

The varieties of the potato can be counted by the hundred. Until the past few years we were mainly dependent upon English cultivators for new varieties, few of which succeeded well in our climate. Our own cultivators have, however, turned their attention to originating new sorts, and with such success as to compete with the English cultivators on their own soil, with varieties combining quality and productiveness. So rapidly does this improvement progress, that it is difficult to keep the run of the new sorts offered for sale. Of those introduced within the past eight years the following deserve especial notice:

Early Rose has retained its position as combining more good qualities than any other early potato. As a later sort, the *Snowflake* promises to be among late potatoes what the *Early Rose* is among early ones. Among the latest varieties that has come out is the *Alpha*, and said to be ten or fifteen days earlier than the *Early Rose*. It is dwarf-growing, and therefore well adapted to garden culture. *Extra Early Vermont*, *Peerless*, *Brownell's Beauty*, *Compton's Surprise* and *Late Rose* are also excellent varieties.

PUMPKIN.

The pumpkin is now seldom cultivated as a garden crop, being entirely superseded as a culinary vegetable by some of the late varieties of squashes, which are superior to it in flavor, sweetness and tenderness of flesh. Their cultivation is similar in all respects to that of winter squashes.

RADISH.

To have radishes in perfection, they should be grown in a light rich soil, so as to induce a rapid growth, which increases their flavor, and renders them crisp and free from stringiness. They can be grown on heavy soils, but are then generally inferior to those grown on light soil.

As they are generally ready to pull for use six weeks after they are sown, they may be sown broadcast, or in intermediate rows between beets, cabbages, early cauliflowers, onions or lettuce, without at all interfering with or producing any injury to the main crop.

Where a regular bed of them is required, a warm, sheltered border may be prepared by manuring, digging and well-pulverizing the soil about the middle of March, or as soon thereafter as the weather permits, and sowing some *Scarlet Short Top* or *Turnip-rooted Radish* seed, either broadcast or in drills about three-quarters of an inch deep and six or eight inches apart. If sown broadcast, the seed should be evenly raked in. To keep up a succession, make sowings at intervals of ten days or a fortnight up to the middle of May. If they are wanted after this, what are known as summer varieties should be sown up to the middle of August. After that, until the first of October, the autumn sorts should be sown, either in separate beds or in the spaces between other vegetables sown during the late summer or early autumn.

If wanted very early, they may be readily grown in frames, sowing the seed about the middle of February, and protecting the frames from frost at night by suitable coverings, giving plenty of air in the middle of the day and watering sparingly. The turnip-rooted sorts are best for growing in frames, as they bulb quickly.

The sorts most generally grown for spring use are the *Long Scarlet Short Top*, the *Red* and the *White Turnip-rooted*, and the *Scarlet Olive-shaped*, the latter being very early and crisp, and to be preferred for the first crop. For summer use, the *Gray* and the *Yellow Turnip-rooted* should be used. They should be used before attaining their full size; they are best when not exceeding an inch in diameter. For winter use, the *Black Spanish*, the *White Spanish*, and the *Rose-colored Chinese* are the best; but they are not generally eaten out of hand, being usually sliced, and served with vinegar and oil as a root salad. These winter varieties can be preserved for winter use by gathering them before frost sets in, cutting off the tops, and packing the roots in boxes filled with earth or sand, and kept in a cellar free from frost. Before using them, they should be soaked in water for an hour or two, in order to restore their crispness.

Another species of radish has of late years come into use. It is known as the *Rat-tailed Radish*, from the appearance of the long seed-pods, which are used for pickling. The pods, when full-grown, are from two to three feet long, but are used when only half grown, tender and succulent. They make a very pleasant, agreeable pickle; they may also be eaten in a raw state, and are excellent stewed or boiled.

RHUBARB.

The rhubarb of our gardens is grown for the leaf stalks, which are used instead of gooseberries for pies, tarts and other culinary purposes.

It requires a very deep, rich soil, and can scarcely be too highly manured or too-deeply cultivated. It is propagated either from seeds or from division of the roots. The seeds should be sown in good rich soil, in April, in drills an inch deep and a foot apart, thinning out the plants, when three or four inches high, to eight or nine inches apart. The ensuing autumn or spring they may be planted out into a permanent bed, which has been trenched two feet deep and very highly manured; the plants being set three feet apart each way. When propagated from established roots, they may be divided, reserving one or more eyes to each division, either in the autumn or in the spring, and planting them in the same way as seedling plants. The after culture consists in keeping the bed clear of weeds, forking in a top dressing of manure every spring, and cutting off the flower stems as they appear. If these are permitted to grow, they weaken the plant and reduce the size of the leaves and leaf stalks. For the same reason no leaves should be gathered the first year and only a few the second year; after that the crop may be more freely gathered. In gathering the leaves, they should be pulled off vertically, and not cut or broken off, as the part left rots and injures the crown of the plant.

Rhubarb may be forwarded and had much earlier in the season, by placing over each plant, in February or March, an empty barrel, and surrounding it with a bed of leaves or long manure two or three feet thick. By this process the stems are blanched, and become very crisp and tender, but lose their flavor to some extent. It scarcely repays the trouble of doing it, except in having an out-of-season luxury.

For family use the large, coarse-growing sorts are not as desirable as those which are of smaller growth, but higher flavor, and more tender and succulent. The following two varieties are the only ones we recommend for private gardens:

Myatt's Linnæus; is an early, medium-sized variety, of fine flavor, and, comparatively with many other sorts, of less acidity.

Early Prince Imperial; is an early medium-sized variety of high flavor; it turns red in cooking, becoming as red as currant jelly, which makes it very desirable for stewing. This is probably the *Prince Albert* of some growers. It is grown about Boston chiefly.

The outer skin of both these varieties is so thin and delicate, that it is not necessary to remove it in preparing it for cooking.

ROCAMBOLE.

This is a vegetable of the onion family, resembling garlic, but having smaller bulbs; it is milder and sweeter flavored than garlic.

It is very hardy, and is increased either by seeds, by separation of the bulbs, or by the rocamboles, or small bulbs produced upon the flower stem of the plant. The seeds may be sown and treated the same as onions. The sets or cloves of the bulb are cultivated in the same way as shallots, described in another place.

RUTA-BAGA.

The ruta-baga, or Swedish turnip, is not really a turnip, but belongs to a different species of the Brassica family. It is analogous to the kohl-rabi, only that the root, and not the stem, is developed into a large fleshy bulb.

It requires a deep, rich, mellow soil, which should be well pulverized before sowing the seed. It delights in a fresh soil, but when manured should have well-rotted manure or fine ground bone. When grown for farming purposes it is sown about the middle of May, but when grown for table use, it may be sown any time during the month of July, as it is not necessary to have as large roots for the kitchen as for stock-feeding, and, besides, the later sown and smaller roots are more succulent and tender.

The drills should be fifteen or sixteen inches apart and half an inch deep. When the plants are in their second or third leaf, they should be thinned out by the hoe to ten or twelve inches apart, giving the soil between the rows a good stirring at the same time, repeating it five or six weeks afterwards, or as often as may be necessary to keep down the weeds.

As the seed germinates very quickly, and is very liable to be eaten off by the turnip fly, the drills, after the seeds are covered in, should be well dusted with soot, lime, or tobacco dust, mixed with an equal quantity of dry ashes, repeating the dusting every morning and evening for a week; a peck a day would suffice for an acre of ground.

There are numerous varieties of the ruta-baga, but the sort best adapted in this country for garden cultivation is the *Improved American*.

SALSIFY OR OYSTER PLANT.

Salsify is sometimes called oyster plant, from a fancied resemblance of the flavor of the root, when cooked, to that of cooked oysters. The roots are white, and resemble small carrots in size and shape.

It requires a good mellow, rich soil, well pulverized to a depth of fourteen or fifteen inches. The seeds should be sown in April or May, in drills an inch deep and twelve to fourteen inches apart. When the plants are two or three inches high, they should be thinned out to six inches apart. The after cultivation is the same as that for parsnips. As the seed does not ripen evenly, much of it does not vegetate; it is therefore necessary to sow it somewhat thickly.

Salsify is quite hardy, and can therefore be left in the ground all winter, but to have a supply during the winter, a sufficient quantity should be taken up late in the autumn, and stored in moist sand or earth in a dry, cool cellar.

The young shoots from plants that have been left out all winter, as they shoot up in the spring, are sometimes cut and used as asparagus, which they somewhat resemble in flavor; but the roots are the part chiefly used for culinary purposes.

There is a popular notion that this vegetable is peculiarly suited for consumptive persons; but whether it is correct or not, we are unable to say. The notion probably arises from the resemblance of its flavor to that of oysters, they being frequently recommended as an article of diet to persons suffering from that disease.

SCOLYMUS.

This vegetable resembles the salsify, and by some is called the Spanish Oyster Plant. It requires the same soil and cultivation as the salsify.

The roots are considered to be very healthful and nutritious, and also are very delicate and pleasant flavored. This vegetable, scorzonera and salsify are not as much cultivated as they ought to be, as they furnish a very agreeable variety to our stock of winter vegetables, and, withal, are of very easy culture.

SCORZONERA.

The roots of this plant closely resemble salsify, but are black on the outside and somewhat smaller. The cultivation is the same as that of salsify or carrots.

The outer black rind of the roots should be scraped off, and the roots soaked in water for two or three hours before cooking them, in order to extract an unpleasant, bitter taste which they otherwise would have. They are then much like salsify in flavor.

SEA-KALE.

This delicious vegetable is not much grown in this country, but is well worth cultivation. It can be grown either from cuttings of the roots or from seeds.

It likes a deep sandy loam, highly manured and well trenched, as its roots penetrate deeply into the soil. The seeds may be sown either in October or early in the spring, in hills two feet apart in row and three feet between the rows. Sow six or eight seeds an inch and a half or two inches deep in each hill, and when the plants are well up, thin them out to three or four in each. When grown from cuttings of the roots, cut up some old roots into pieces three or four inches long, and plant, in March or April, three or four inches deep, in hills, as directed for those grown from seeds. They may also be grown in rows three feet apart, and the plants set eighteen inches apart on the row. In this case it is well to sow the seeds or plant the cuttings in a nursery bed, setting them, or thinning them out to six or eight inches apart, and transplanting them the following spring.

In the autumn, when the leaves have decayed, the plants should have a covering, four to six inches thick, of manure, leaves or sea-weed; this protects them from the bad effects of freezing and thawing, and causes them to start earlier in the spring. When the frost is out of the ground, this may be taken off, or, if rotten enough, may be forked in. The plants are then to be covered to a depth of ten or twelve inches with sand, peat or some similar material, to blanch the shoots as they grow. Some invert large garden pots over the plants and blanch them in that way. In three or four weeks after this is done the shoots will probably be fit to cut; but this should not be done until they are four or five inches in length. The cutting may be continued until the flower heads form, and these may be used as broccoli after they have made some growth in the open air, when they form a small head resembling a broccoli or a cauliflower.

The cutting should not be too close, especially for the first year or two, as it has a tendency to weaken the plants. It is well to only blanch every other row each year, in order that the plants may have an opportunity to recuperate, for strong roots can only be had by strong, healthy foliage. To the same end, the plants should never be allowed to go to seed. Sea-kale, like asparagus, is a seashore plant—hence a top dressing of salt, as directed for the latter vegetable, is of service to it.

There are no varieties of it.

SHALLOT.

The shallot is a species of onion, the root of which is composed of numerous small bulbs, united at their base and covered with a thin skin. It is chiefly used in a green state, early in the spring.

It thrives in any soil suitable for the onion, preferring, however, a light, warm soil. It is chiefly grown by dividing the bulbs and planting the offsets. These should be planted with a dibble or trowel, in rows twelve inches apart, and four to six inches distant on the rows, the holes being two or three inches deep. When wanted for early spring use, they are planted towards the end of August or early in September, and are left in the open ground all winter. They may also be planted in April for later use. When the tops die off, the bulbs should be taken up, well dried, and kept in a warm, dry place; damp and cold cause them to decay rapidly.

There are five or six varieties, but none of them are better than the common sort.

SORREL.

Sorrel is used abroad, especially in Germany and France, as freely as spinach is with us. It is considered to be a very healthful vegetable, of strong alterative powers, and of great service to those who live largely on salt provisions.

The seed should be sown in April or May, in drills half an inch deep and fifteen to eighteen inches apart. The young plants should be thinned out to ten or twelve inches apart, and by July or August the leaves will be fit to cut. When the flower stems show themselves, they should be cut out, so as to encourage the development of the leaves.

The plant is perennial, and thrives in any good moist garden soil. In winter it is well to give it a light protection of strawy stable manure, forking it in early in the spring.

There are several varieties of it, but the sort most generally esteemed in Paris is the *Belleville*, or *Broad-leaved Sorrel*.

SKIRRET.

This vegetable, though formerly much esteemed, is now not much cultivated, being superseded by salsify and scorzonera, to which it is fully equal, if not superior. It has much the taste of a parsnip, and by many is preferred to it. The roots are the parts used; they are of a russet color on the outside, and white within, and when well grown are six or eight inches long and about an inch in diameter.

It succeeds best in a light, mellow, moist soil. The seeds, which sometimes take four or five weeks to vegetate, should be sown early in April, in drills a foot apart and an inch deep. The plants should be thinned out to five or six inches apart. The after culture is the same as for salsify. In September or October the roots will be fit for use. Those required for winter use should be taken up before frost sets in, packed in sand, and kept in a cool, dry cellar.

There are no varieties of it.

SPINACH.

Spinach, to be grown in perfection, requires a very highly manured soil, so as to make it develop large succulent leaves. It can be grown both as an early spring and a summer crop. When taken off in the spring, it leaves the soil in excellent condition, without any further manuring, for beets, carrots, parsnips or turnips.

For spring use, the seed should be thinly sown from the first to the end of September, in well prepared soil, in drills an inch deep and a foot apart. When cold weather sets in it should have a slight covering of straw or salt hay, more to prevent the effects of freezing and thawing than to protect it from frost, as it is quite hardy. For summer use the seed should be sown in March or April. Some gardeners sow it between their rows of early cabbages, as it becomes fit to cut in five or six weeks after being sown. To assist it in making a rapid growth it should be frequently hoed.

If wanted during the winter, it may be cut on a mild day, sprinkled with water, put into a box or barrel, and placed in a cool but not freezing cellar. In this way it may be kept for ten days or a fortnight.

There are several varieties, but the best two for private gardens are the *Flanders* and the *Large Prickly-seeded*. The first is very bushy and produces very large leaves;

the plants should be thinned out to six or eight inches apart. The last, not producing such large leaves, should be thinned out to four or five inches apart. It is also slower in running to seed than the *Flanders*.

SQUASH.

Squash seeds should be sown in May or June, in hills, as directed for cucumbers and melons, their after culture being the same. The bush sorts should be sown in hills three or four feet apart; the running sorts in hills six to ten feet apart, according to the nature of their growth. Five or six seeds should be sown in each hill, and care be had to keep off the striped bug; after the plants are past danger they may be thinned out to two or three plants in a hill.

For early use the *White* and the *Yellow Scalloped Bush* varieties, with the *Summer Bush* crook-necked, are the best. For late summer, autumn and winter use, the *Boston Marrow*, the *Turban* or *Acorn*, the *Yokohama* and the *Hubbard* are the best, the latter keeping into the late spring.

In keeping winter squashes, it is absolutely necessary that they should be kept from cold or dampness, and the flower end should never be set under, as they soon decay when this is not exposed to the air.

SWEET POTATO.

The sweet potato requires a light, warm, rich soil; in heavy soils it does not succeed. In this latitude it is propagated by planting the tubers, in April, in a moderate hot-bed. The tubers, uncut, should be placed three or four inches apart, with two or three inches of sand or soil under them, and covered with three inches of light, rich soil. In about a month they will start into growth, and when the shoots or sprouts are about four inches long above the ground, they may be taken off and transplanted into the open ground. The tubers will throw up a succession of shoots, so that three or four sets of them can be had for planting.

The sprouts may either be set out in ridges or in hills. In the former case, the rows should be four feet apart, and the plants twelve or fifteen inches apart on the row. When planted in hills, they should be four feet apart each way, allowing three plants to a hill, putting a shovelful of rotted manure in each hill. The sprouts should be set one-third to one-half their entire length and watered when set out, continuing the watering occasionally if the weather is dry. They should be kept clear of weeds until the plants begin to cover the ground.

A hot-bed, five feet square, planted in April with tubers, will furnish enough of plants to yield twelve or fifteen bushels of potatoes. They may be set out towards the end of May or any time during the month of June. To preserve them in winter, they should be stored in boxes or barrels with sand, and kept in a warm, dry place; cold and damp cause them to decay.

There are eight or nine varieties; but for cultivation in our northern latitudes, the *Nansemond*, a yellow sort, and the *Red-skinned*, are the best two. They are hardier and earlier than most of the other sorts.

SWISS CHARD.

This is a species of beet, producing large, strong leaves with thick midribs, and small roots not useful for culinary purposes. The thin portions of the leaves, and the leaves themselves, when young, are used as greens or spinach, and the midribs as asparagus. It withstands the heat of our summers, and is a very useful vegetable, not as much grown as it should be.

The soil should be tolerably rich, so as to encourage a quick, succulent growth. The seed may be sown any time in April or May, in drills eighteen inches apart and an inch and a half deep. When the plants are about three inches high, they should be thinned out to ten or twelve inches apart, and treated like the common red beet.

There are five or six sorts, but the best is the *Silver-leaved*, or true *Swiss Chard*.

TARRAGON.

Tarragon is a hardy perennial plant, grown chiefly for its leaves and the tips of the young shoots, which are chiefly used for flavoring stews, soups, salads, pickles and vinegar. As it seldom produces seeds, it is generally propagated by division of the roots. These should be set out in any good garden soil, in April, in rows fifteen inches apart, and the plants set ten or twelve inches apart on the row, covering the sets two or three inches deep.

If seed can be obtained, it should be sown in April or May, in a cold frame or in a nursery bed. The drills should be six or eight inches apart, and when the plants are three or four inches high they should be set out as directed for the roots.

TOMATO.

To have tomatoes early in the season, it is necessary to sow the seed in drills six inches apart and half an inch deep, in a moderate hot-bed, early in the month of March. In four or five weeks the plants may be transplanted into a frame four to six inches apart, and will then make nice, stocky plants for setting out in the open ground about the middle of May. Where there is not the convenience of a hot-bed, the seeds may be sown in a box, covered with a pane of glass, and set in a kitchen window; these will come forward nearly as fast as when sown in a hot-bed.

For later use, the seeds may be sown in the open ground, in a warm, sheltered border, early in May, when the plants will be ready to transplant early in June.

They should be planted in hills from three to four feet apart each way, a spadeful of well-rotted manure being mixed in each hill. Some persons train them on lath trellises, some stake them with pea-brush, and others train them within hoops, all of which give an amount of trouble which the generality of people do not like to incur. In order to keep the fruit clean, to prevent its rotting and to forward its ripening, it is necessary to keep it from laying in direct contact with the earth; this is easily done by laying around the hills a thickness of two or three inches of small twig brush, which will keep the fruit from the soil. When the plants are about a foot high, they should be earthed up.

The varieties are very numerous, and every season one or more new sorts are introduced to public notice as being superior to any that have preceded them, but not one in ten becomes a standard sort. The best early variety is the *Early Smooth Red;* for the general crop the *Trophy* is the best; for making catsup or preserving, we think highly of the *Feejee,* or *Lester's Perfected,* as it is very solid, contains less fluid than any other sort, and is of most excellent flavor. It is quite a late sort. For pickling, the *Pear-shaped* and the *Yellow Plum* are the best.

To get or keep an early yield of any variety of tomato, the first ripened fruits should be reserved for seed.

TURNIP.

To have early turnips, the seed should be sown from early in April until the middle of May, in drills half an inch deep and twelve to fifteen inches apart, the plants being thinned out to six or eight inches apart. For the early crops the soil should be warm and light, but the late crops can be grown on heavy soil. In either case the land must be well manured. For the autumn crops, the seed can be sown from the end of July until the end of August. About a month after the plants are up they should be well hoed, and the operation repeated in three or four weeks afterwards, as this makes them grow rapidly.

There are a great number of varieties of turnips, but for general use, both for an early crop as well as for a late crop, there is none equal to the *Red-topped Strap-leaved* among the white-fleshed sorts, and the *Golden Ball* and the *Yellow Finland* among the yellow-fleshed sorts.

WATER-CRESS.

Water-cress requires a clear running stream and a gravelly soil. The roots should be planted in the spring of the year in slow-running streams, where the water is from three to eight inches deep. When the roots are well established the plants will rapidly increase, and, by their natural process of seed-sowing and spreading of the roots, they will soon cover the surface of the stream. When planted, the rows should be planted parallel with the course of the stream, about eighteen inches apart. The plants should always be cut, not broken off, as breaking them off is injurious to the plants. After they have been cut off two or three times, they will begin to stock out or thicken out, and then the oftener they are cut the better.

When raised from seeds they should be sown on the margin of the stream, and when of suitable size transplanted into it, where it is an inch and a half or two inches deep. The most suitable time for sowing is in the months of April, May and June.

There are said to be three varieties of water-cress—namely: the *Green-leaved*, which is considered to be the easiest to cultivate; the *Small Brown-leaved*, which is thought to be the hardiest, and the *Large Brown-leaved*, which is said to be the best for deep water.

WATER-MELON.

The water-melon succeeds best in light, sandy soils, heavy soils inducing too much leaf growth. The cultivation is the same as that of the musk-melon, only that the hills should be at least eight feet apart each way, and only two plants in each hill. The seeds should not be sown until May, or until settled warm weather has set in.

There are numerous sorts, of which the *Mountain Sweet* and the *Black Spanish* are the best for table use. The citron is grown exclusively for preserving purposes.

POT HERBS.

In most garden books directions are given for the cultivation of aromatic, pot, sweet and medicinal herbs. We shall, however, confine ourselves to pot herbs, or those grown exclusively for culinary uses. They are *Sweet Basil, Sweet Fennel, Sweet Marjoram, Spear Mint, Sage, Summer Savory* and *Broad-leaved Thyme*.

They all require the same general cultivation, which consists in sowing the seeds, during April or May, in rich, mellow soil, in drills half an inch deep and a foot apart. As the seeds of most of them are very small, the bed in which they are sown should be shaded until the plants come up, and kept scrupulously clean of weeds. By the middle or end of June the plants will be fit to set out into the permanent beds, in rows twelve to fifteen inches apart, and the plants eight to ten inches apart on the rows.

All herbs should be gathered just before they begin to flower, as then they have their flavor and aroma most highly developed. They should be tied in small bunches and dried in the shade under cover.

In designating each herb above, we have indicated which is the best variety of each.

MONTHLY REMINDERS.

JANUARY.—As this is the dead of winter, not much can be done in garden operations, except in preparation for the ensuing season. The collection of manure and its preparation should be attended to. It should always be kept well stacked up, and not allowed to be carelessly left loose, and so to become frozen.

Air the cold frames whenever the weather permits. If they are covered with snow, it should be removed, unless the soil in the frame is frozen. If that is the case, they may remain covered up for two or three weeks without injury.

Prepare pea-brush, etc., and see that your garden tools are in good order.

FEBRUARY.—Attend to the manure piles, turning them over once or twice to facilitate their decomposition.

Make up hot-beds, and towards the end of the month sow in them cabbage, egg plant, lettuce, peppers and tomato seeds. See that the cold frames are properly attended to.

Broad beans and cabbage seed may be sown in cold frames—the latter when a hot-bed is not to be had.

Repair sashes, frames, protection boxes, etc.

MARCH.—Hot-beds may still be made, and seeds of tender vegetables sown in them, as directed for last month. Plant wintered-over lettuce in cold frames, when it is desired to have them sooner than they can be had in the open air. Radishes, also, can be sown in cold frames for the same purpose.

If the ground should be in suitable condition, it may now be manured and spaded. Towards the end of the month, in warm, dry soils, sow cabbage, carrot, lettuce, celery for early crops, radishes, turnips, spinach, broad beans, leeks, beets and peas in a sheltered border. Plant horse-radish, rocambole, onion sets and chives.

Make plantations of asparagus, rhubarb, sea-kale and artichokes. Top dress old beds of them with short manure, forking it in lightly close to the plants.

Roots of carrots, beets, parsnips, onions and leeks, with cabbages and celery intended for seed, may be planted out towards the end of the month in dry, warm soils, but if the land is heavy or wet, defer it until next month. The crowns of these roots should be protected from frost by drawing some earth over them, and removing it in April.

As the sun now begins to have some power, particular attention must be paid to the hot-beds and cold frames to prevent the plants scorching. Air must be freely given if the weather is spring-like, and some shading may be required in the middle of the day. Water them if it is needed, using tepid water.

APRIL.—Plant asparagus, rhubarb, sea-kale and artichokes, if not done previously. Divide roots of tarragon, chives, and any perennial medicinal or sweet herbs. Plant out cabbage, cauliflower—protecting it—broad beans, horse-radish, onion sets, lettuce, Jerusalem artichoke, potatoes, and start sweet potatoes in a hot-bed. Plant out roots of esculents intended for seed raising. Sow beet, cabbage, onions, peas, radishes, spinach, lettuce, turnips, endive, cardoon, carrot, celery, cress, leeks, rhubarb, artichoke, asparagus, mustard, nasturtium, salsify, scorzonera, sea-kale, skirret, chervil, patience, kohl-rabi, tomatoes, parsley and sweet herbs. Sow cucumbers and melons in frames, and towards the end of the month bush beans and Indian corn out-of-doors. Hoe crops already planted, in order to destroy the weeds, which now begin to germinate and start into growth.

See that the hot-beds and cold frames are well aired, shaded if necessary, watered and protected at night.

MAY.—Thin out the early sown crops of beets, parsnips, carrots, etc. Transplant cabbage, lettuce, egg plants, tomatoes, peppers, etc., from the hot-beds, frames and warm border seed beds. The sowing of any seeds that were neglected last month should now be attended to without delay.

Sow borecole, brussels sprouts, broccoli, cauliflower, cabbage, beans, endive, carrot, cress, cucumber, melon, water-melon, squash, nasturtium, martynia, okra, peas, sweet corn, pumpkin, tomato, radish and sweet herbs. Plant potatoes, sweet potatoes, and any plants still remaining in the frames or hot-beds.

Water all newly transplanted plants at the time of transplanting, and two or three times afterwards if the weather is dry, or until the plants are established.

Keep the hoe going in order to destroy the weeds, which will now begin to be troublesome.

JUNE.—Early crops, such as lettuce, radishes, spinach, etc., when gathered, may be succeeded by late beets and carrots. Sow them, and also bush beans, cucumbers, endive, sweet corn, pumpkin, squash and okra. Transplant cabbage and celery for summer use; also leeks and cardoons; and plant potatoes and sweet potatoes.

Water early cauliflowers as they begin to head.

Hoe and thin out all standing crops.

JULY.—Transplant cabbage, cardoons, celery, endive,

leeks, peppers, etc., for autumn crops. Sow bush beans and pole beans, cucumbers for pickling, endive, kohl-rabi, summer radish, ruta-baga. and, towards the end of the month, turnips. Potatoes may be planted early in the month.

Sweet herbs should be cut and dried this month.

AUGUST.—Celery may be transplanted up to the 15th. Sow turnips, fetticus, bush beans for pickling, onion seed to stand the winter, lettuce for autumn use, and spinach for an early crop. Onions will be ripe this month, and should be pulled and dried.

SEPTEMBER.—The fall crops will now be growing rapidly, and will require hoeing and other attention. From the 10th to the 20th sow cabbage, cauliflower and lettuce seed for young plants to winter over in cold frames. Shallots and onions should be planted, and spinach and German greens sown for next spring's crop. Earth up such celery as may be wanted for next month.

OCTOBER.—Earth up celery, dig up potatoes and other roots, as they mature, and store them away for use. Collect squashes and pumpkins, and expose them, in a dry place, to a good airing, previous to stowing them away. Blanch endive, hoe and weed out fetticus and spinach, plant out cabbage and lettuce plants in cold frames.

NOVEMBER.—All vegetables not secured for storing away should now be attended to. Spinach, lettuce out-of-doors, fetticus and outdoor onions should be protected by coverings of straw, salt hay or cedar brush. Short horse dung is best for the onions. Clear up and dig all ground as the crops are taken off, as it prevents delay in commencing in the spring.

Put the sashes on such of the cold frames as have been

filled with cabbage or lettuce plants, giving air freely by taking the sashes entirely off on sunny or mild days.

DECEMBER.—Attend to the celery that has been stored away in trenches for winter use; cover it little by little. Protect spinach, onions, shallots, kale, etc., that were sown in September, and cover rhubarb, sea-kale, asparagus, artichokes, etc., with five or six inches' thickness of long, coarse manure.

Store away pea-brush, and other materials of the kind, from the weather. Commence to collect manure and to prepare compost heaps. Give air to the cold frames on sunny days.

DICK'S
RECITATIONS AND READINGS.

A carefully compiled Series of Volumes, uniform in size and style, which will include everything that is fresh and popular, introducing also the older Gems of the English Language that are always in demand: embracing

CHARACTER SKETCHES,   **DIALECT PIECES,**
HUMOROUS,   **SENTIMENTAL,**
PATHETIC,   **PATRIOTIC,**
ELOQUENT,   **AND**   **SERIOUS**

Recitations and Readings in Poetry and Prose, excluding everything that is not eminently appropriate, either for Declamation or Public Reading.

Each Number contains about 180 Pages of Reading Matter, printed on fine paper, from clear type, and handsomely bound in Illuminated Paper Cover, Price,   30 Cents. Or Full Cloth, - - - - - 50 "

DICK & FITZGERALD, Publishers,

Copies sent per mail, free of postage, on receipt of price.   18 Ann Street, New York.

Nos. 1, 2, 3 and 4 of this Series ARE NOW READY.

DICK & FITZGERALD,

PUBLISHERS, NEW YORK.

₊ The Publishers, upon receipt of the price, will send any of the following books by mail, POSTAGE FREE, to any part of the United States. In ordering books, the full name, post office, county and State should be plainly written.

Dick's Encyclopedia of Practical Receipts and Processes. Containing over 6,400 Receipts; embracing thorough information, in plain language, applicable to almost every possible industrial and domestic requirement. The scope of this work is different from any other book of the kind. The contents of the Encyclopedia are collated from works on the various subjects by authors of eminence in their respective branches, divested of technicalities, simplified and illustrated by diagrams, where necessary, so as to make the whole plain and intelligible to the uninitiated. This work presents a complete and indispensable book for the household, farm, garden, &c.; including instructions as to what to do and how to do it, in case of all accidents, contingencies, and ailments of daily life. It also affords a valuable Book of Reference for the Druggist, enabling him to make up a number of "Sundries," especially Toilet Soaps, Dentifrices, Cosmetics, and Perfumery; also specific Medicines and Remedies derived from the practice of eminent Physicians, or from various European officinal sources; thus forming a useful and desirable adjunct to the United States Pharmacopœia. It enables the Grocer to prepare his own Flavoring Extracts, Vinegar, and a host of other articles, cheaper and better than he can purchase them; and to test the quality of some of the Goods that he buys and sells. To the Liquor Dealer it gives the best and latest methods of treating and improving his liquors; of preparing Cordials, &c.; of making, managing, and bottling all kinds of Wines, Cider, &c.,—it lays before the workman the results obtained by the experiments and experience of the masters of his trade. In fact it is almost useless to attempt an enumeration of the advantages of this work, as there is scarcely a branch of Industry that may not derive information and profit from its pages. The Index of this work occupies 42 three-column pages, in small type. 600 pages, royal octavo, cloth.
Price ....$5.00.
Bound in half calf, extra..$7.50.
☞ Full descriptive circular of the above sent, by mail, free.

Ferrero's Art of Dancing without a Master; *or, Ball-Room Guide and Instructor.* To which is added Hints on Etiquette; also, the Figures, Music, and necessary instructions for the most modern and improved Dances. By Edward Ferrero. This work contains 105 pages of the choicest Music, arranged for the Piano-forte by the most celebrated professors. The Music alone is worth ten times the price of the book.
Bound in boards, with cloth back. Price................................75 cts.
In paper cover...50 cts.

Wilson's Book of Recitations and Dialogues. With Instructions in Elocution and Declamation. Containing a choice selection of Poetical and Prose Recitations and Original Colloquies. Designed as a Reading Book for Classes, and as an Assistant to Teachers and Students in preparing Exhibitions. By Floyd B. Wilson, Professor of Elocution. The Colloquies are entirely original. Paper cover. Price................30 cts.
Bound in boards, cloth back...50 cts.

Popular Books sent Free of Postage at the Prices annexed.

The Parlor Magician; *or, One Hundred Tricks for the Drawing-Room,* containing an Extensive and Miscellaneous Collection of Conjuring and Legerdemain; Sleights with Dice, Dominoes, Cards, Ribbons, Rings, Fruit, Coin, Balls, Handkerchiefs, etc., all of which may be performed in the Parlor or Drawing-Room, without the aid of any apparatus; also embracing a choice variety of Curious Deceptions, which may be performed with the aid of simple apparatus; the whole illustrated and clearly explained with 121 engravings. Paper Covers. Price.................30 cts.
Bound in boards, with cloth back.................................50 cts

Book of Riddles and Five Hundred Home Amusements. Containing a Choice and Curious Collection of Riddles, Charades, Enigmas, Rebuses, Anagrams, Transpositions, Conundrums, Amusing Puzzles, Queer Sleights, Recreations in Arithmetic, Fireside Games and Natural Magic, embracing Entertaining Amusements in Magnetism, Chemistry, Second Sight and Simple Recreations in Science for Family and Social Pastime, illustrated with sixty Engravings. Paper covers. Price.............30 cts.
Bound in boards, with cloth back.................................50 cts.

Book of Fireside Games. Containing an Explanation of the most Entertaining Games suited to the Family Circle as a Recreation, such as Games of Action, Games which merely require attention, Games which require memory, Catch Games, which have for their objects Tricks or Mystification, Games in which an opportunity is afforded to display Gallantry, Wit, or some slight knowledge of certain Sciences, Amusing Forfeits, Fireside Games for Winter Evening Amusement, etc.
Paper covers. Price...30 cts.
Bound in boards, with cloth back.................................50 cts.

Parlor Theatricals; *or, Winter Evenings' Entertainment.* Containing Acting Proverbs, Dramatic Charades, Acting Charades, or Drawing-Room Pantomimes, Musical Burlesques, Tableaux Vivants, etc.; with Instructions for Amateurs; how to Construct a Stage and Curtain; how to get up Costumes and Properties; on the "Making up" of Characters; Exits and Entrances; how to arrange Tableaux, etc. Illustrated with Engravings. Paper covers. Price..............................30 cts.
Bound in boards, cloth back......................................50 cts.

The Book of 500 Curious Puzzles. Containing a large collection of entertaining Paradoxes, Perplexing Deceptions in numbers, and Amusing Tricks in Geometry. By the author of "The Sociable," "The Secret Out," "The Magician's Own Book." Illustrated with a great variety of Engravings. This book commands a large sale. It will furnish fun and amusement for a whole winter. Paper covers. Price..............30 cts
Bound in boards, with cloth back.................................50 cts.
The above five books are compiled from the "Sociable" and "Magician's Own."

The American Boys' Book of Sports and Games. A Repository of In and Out-Door Amusements for Boys and Youth. Illustrated with nearly 700 engravings, designed by White, Herrick, Weir and Harvey, and engraved by N. Orr. This is, unquestionably, the most attractive and valuable book of its kind ever issued in this or any other country. It has been three years in preparation, and embraces all the sports and games that tend to develop the physical constitution, improve the mind and heart, and relieve the tedium of leisure hours, both in the parlor and the field. The Engravings are all in the finest style of art, and embrace eight full-page ornamental titles, illustrating the several departments of the work, beautifully printed on tinted paper. The book is issued in the best style, being printed on fine sized paper, and handsomely bound. Extra cloth, gilt side and back, extra gold. Price................................$3 50
Extra cloth, full gilt edges, back and side......................$4 00

Popular Books sent Free of Postage at the Prices annexed.

McBride's All Kinds of Dialogues. A Collection of Original Humorous and Domestic Dialogues, introducing Yankee, French, Irish, Dutch, and other characters. Excellently adapted for Amateur performance. By H. Elliott McBride. This book constitutes a second series of McBride's Comic Dialogues, and affords an additional variety of the spirited dialogues and short dramatic scenes contained in the latter book. They are all entirely original, and develop in a marked degree the eccentricities and peculiarities of the various ideal, but genuine, characters which are represented in them. They are specially adapted for School Exhibitions and all other celebrations where the success of the entertainment is partly or entirely dependent on the efforts of the young folks.
Illuminated Paper Cover, Price..30 cts.
Bound in Boards..50 cts.

Beecher's Recitations and Readings. Humorous, Serious, Dramatic; including Prose and Poetical Selections in Dutch, French, Yankee, Irish, Backwoods, Negro and other Dialects. Edited by Alvah C. Beecher. This excellent selection has been compiled to meet a growing demand for Public Readings, and contains a number of the favorite pieces that have been rendered with telling effect by the most popular Public Readers of the present time. It includes, also, choice selections for Recitation, and is, therefore, admirably adapted for use at Evening Entertainments, School Celebrations, and other Festival occasions.
16mo. Illuminated Paper Cover, Price.............................30 cts.
Bound in Boards..50 cts.

Day's Cards for Popping the Question. An Original Game for Lovers and Sweethearts, or for Merry-Making in a Party of Young People. These cards are not only delightfully useful to diffident lovers—enabling them to realize deferred hopes, and cure aching hearts, but will make lots of fun and innocent amusement in a party of young people, often resulting in earnest love passages begun in sport—preventing shyness and diffidence, and promoting that healthy and easy confidence between the sexes so necessary in all social meetings. The set consists of forty-two Cards, viz: twenty-one questions, which are mostly earnest declarations of love, and twenty-one answers, equally pithy and to the point. As soon as these Cards become known we feel sure that they will have an endless sale. Put up in cases, with directions for playing. Price..................30 cts.

Ned Turner's Circus Joke Book. A Collection of the best Jokes, Bon Mots, Repartees, Gems of Wit, and Funny Sayings and Doings of the celebrated Equestrian Clown and Ethiopian Comedian, Ned Turner. Arranged and compiled by George E. Gowan. This book forms the third of the series by this versatile popular performer. Price.............10 cts.

Chips from Uncle Sam's Jack-Knife. Illustrated with over 165 Comical Engravings, and comprising a collection of over 500 Laughable Stories, Funny Adventures, Comic Poetry, Queer Conundrums, Terrific Puns, Witty Sayings, Sublime Jokes and Sentimental Sentences. The whole being a most perfect portfolio for those who love to laugh.
Large octavo. Price...25 cts.

Clarence Bolton. A New York story, with city life in all its phases. This is one of those fascinating tales of city life that gives an insight into every class of society. Price..............................25 cts.

Grace Weldon; or, *The Pretty Milliner*. This is a story about the Sewing Girls of Boston. Full of fun and adventure. Any person who desires to read a lively story should not fail to get this work.
Price...25 cts.

Popular Books Sent Free of Postage at the Prices annexed.

Howard's Recitations. *Comic, Serious and Pathetic.* Being a collection of fresh Recitations in Prose and Poetry, suitable for Anniversaries, Exhibitions, Sociables and Evening Parties. 180 pages, 16mo.
Paper Cover..............30cts.   Bound in Boards...........50cts.

Frost's New Book of Dialogues. Being an entirely new and original series of Humorous Dialogues, designed for performance at School Anniversaries and Exhibitions. 180 pages. Paper Covers..........30cts.
Bound in Boards...50cts.

Frost's Dialogues for Young Folks. A collection of Original, Moral and Humorous Dialogues, adapted to the use of School and Church Exhibitions, Family Gatherings and Juvenile Celebrations on all occasions. A few of the Dialogues are long enough to form a sort of little drama that will interest more advanced scholars, while short and easy ones abound for the use of quite young children. Paper Cover....................30cts.
Bound in Boards, with Cloth Backs, Side in Colors................50cts.

Frost's Humorous and Exhibition Dialogues. This is a collection of Sprightly Original Dialogues, in Prose and Verse, intended to be spoken at School Exhibitions. Some of the pieces are for boys, some for girls, while a number are designed to be used by both sexes. 180 pages.
Paper Covers..............30cts.   Bound in Boards...........50cts.

French Self-Taught. A new system on the most simple principles for Universal Self-Tuition, with English Pronunciation of every word. By FRANZ THIMM. Price..25cts.

German Self-Taught. Uniform with "French Self-Taught."
By FRANZ THIMM. Price..25cts.

Spanish Self-Taught. Uniform with "French Self-Taught."
By FRANZ THIMM. Price..25cts.

Italian Self-Taught. Uniform with "French Self-Taught."
By FRANZ THIMM. Price..25cts.

Franz Thimm's Modern Languages. Being the above four works bound together in cloth, 16mo. Price.........................$1.50

The Banjo, and How to Play It. Containing, in addition to the Elementary Study, a choice collection of Polkas, Waltzes, Solos, Schottisches, Songs, Hornpipes, Jigs. Reels, &c.; with full explanations of both the "Banjo" and "Guitar" styles of execution, and designed to impart a complete knowledge of the Art of Playing the Banjo practically, without the aid of a Teacher. By FRANK CONVERSE, author of the "Banjo without a Master." 16mo. Bound in Boards, with Cloth Back...............50cts.

How to Speak in Public; *or, the Art of Extempore Oratory.* A valuable manual for those who desire to become ready, off-hand speakers. 16mo. Paper Cover..25cts.

How to Shine in Society; *or, the Science of Conversation.* Containing the principles, laws, and general usages of polite society. 16mo.
Paper Cover..25cts.

The Athlete's Guide. A hand-book on Walking, Running, and Rowing, giving full instructions for Training, and a Record of all the principal events since the year 1773, with sketches of the lives of the most celebrated Athletes. By W. E. HARDING, Ex-Champion. 18mo, cloth. Price.50cts

Popular Books sent Free of Postage at the Prices annexed.

Delisser's Horseman's Guide. Comprising the Laws on Warranty, and the Rules in purchasing and selling Horses, with the decisions and reports of various courts in Europe and the United States; to which is added a detailed account of what constitute soundness and unsoundness, and a precise method simply laid down, for the examination of horses, showing their age to thirty years old; together with an exposure of the various tricks and impositions practiced by low horse-dealers (jockeys) on inexperienced persons; also a valuable Table of each and every bone in the structure of the Horse. The entire matter carefully compiled from Twenty English, Five American, Six French, and Nine German Veterinary Authors, with the opinions of the compiler attached. By George P. Delisser, V. S. & L A., and late Examining Veterinary Surgeon to the American Society for the Prevention of Cruelty to Animals. Bound in boards, cloth back.... 75 cts. Bound in Cloth. Price..$1.00.

Howard's Book of Conundrums and Riddles. Containing over 1,400 Witty Conundrums, Queer Riddles, Perplexing Puzzles, Ingenious Enigmas, Clever Charades, Curious Catches, and Amusing Sells, original and newly dressed. This splendid collection of curious paradoxes will afford the material for a never-ending feast of fun and amusement. Any person, with the assistance of this book, may take the lead in entertaining a company and keeping them in roars of laughter for hours together. It is an invaluable companion for a Picnic or Summer Excursion of any kind, and is just the thing to make a fireside circle merry on a long winter's evening. There is not a poor riddle in the book, the majority being fresh and of the highest order. Paper cover. Price................30 cts. Bound in boards, cloth back. Price.........................50 cts.

Frost's Book of Tableaux and Shadow Pantomimes. Containing a choice collection of Tableaux or living Pictures, embracing Moving Tableaux, Mother Goose Tableaux, Fairy Tale Tableaux Charade and Proverb Tableaux; together with directions for arranging the stage, costuming the characters, and forming appropriate groups. By Miss S. Annie Frost. To which is added a number of Shadow Acts and Pantomimes, with complete stage instructions. 180 pages, paper cover...30 cts. Bound in boards, cloth back..................................50 cts.

Laughing Gas. An Encyclopædia of Wit, Wisdom, and Wind. By Sam Slick, Jr. Comically illustrated with 100 original and laughable Engravings, and nearly 500 side-extending Jokes, and other things to get fat on; and the best thing of it is, that everything about the book is new and fresh—all new—new designs, new stories, new type—no comic almanac stuff. Price...............................25 cts.

The Egyptian Dream Book and Fortune-Teller. Containing an Alphabetical List of Dreams, and numerous methods of Telling Fortunes, including the celebrated Oraculum of Napoleon Bonaparte. Illustrated with explanatory diagrams. Boards, cloth back. Price...40 cts.

Ned Turner's Black Jokes. A collection of Funny Stories, Jokes and Conundrums, interspersed with Witty Sayings and Humorous Dialogues. As given by Ned Turner, the Celebrated Ethiopian Delineator and Equestrian Clown. Price........................10 cts.

Ned Turner's Clown Joke Book. Containing the best Jokes and Gems of Wit, composed and delivered by the favorite Equestrian Clown and Ethiopian Comedian, Ned Turner. 18mo. Price............10 cts.

Sam Slick in Search of a Wife. 12mo. Paper cover. Price...75 cts

Popular Books sent Free of Postage at the Prices annexed.

The Art and Etiquette of Making Love.

A Manual of Love, Courtship and Matrimony. Containing sensible advice in relation to all the delicate situations and perplexing circumstances incidental to the tender passion from the commencement of a courtship until after marriage; together with the duties to be fulfilled and the points of etiquette to be observed by bridesmaids and groomsmen, and all other details of the wedding ceremony; with many curious things concerning matrimony and its consequences; including a complete system of love telegraphy and handkerchief flirtations, and a choice collection of sensible letters, suitable for all the contingencies of love and courtship; also, practical remarks on bashfulness, its prevention and cure. If young ladies or gentlemen want to know:

How to cure bashfulness,
How to commence a courtship,
How to carry on a handkerchief flirtation,
How to please a sweetheart or lover,
How to write a love-letter,
How to "pop the question,"
How to act before and after a proposal,
How to accept or reject a proposal,
How to break off an engagement,
How to act after an engagement,
How to act as bridesmaid or groomsman,
How the etiquette of a wedding and the after reception should be observed,

And in fact, how to fulfill every duty, and meet every contingency connected with courtship and matrimony, they will find it all clearly explained in this book. Large 16mo., 176 pages, paper cover. Price..................30 cts.
Bound in boards, cloth back. Price..................50 cts.

The Amateur Trapper and Trap-Maker's Guide.

A complete and carefully prepared treatise on the art of Trapping, Snaring and Netting; containing plain directions for constructing the most approved Traps, Snares, Nets, and Dead-Falls; the best methods of applying them to their various purposes; and the most successful Baits for attracting all kinds of Animals, Birds, &c., with their special uses in each case; introducing, also, practical receipts for preparing Skins and Furs for Market, and for Tanning them for future use; with concise but comprehensive instructions for Preserving and Stuffing specimens of Birds and Animals in the most natural and durable manner. The entire work is based on the experience of the most successful Trappers, and on information derived from other authentic professional sources. By Stanley Harding. This comprehensive work is embellished with fifty well drawn and engraved illustrations; and these, together with the clear explanations which accompany them, will enable anybody of moderate comprehension to make and set any of the traps described. It also gives the baits usually employed by the most successful Hunters and Trappers, and exposes their secret methods of attracting and catching animals, birds, &c., with scarcely a possibility of failure. Large 16mo., paper covers. Price..................50 cts.
Bound in boards, cloth back..................75 cts.

Very Little Dialogues for Very Little Folks.

Containing forty-seven new and original dialogues, with short and easy parts, almost entirely in words of one syllable, suited to the capacity and comprehension of very young children. This work has been issued because it was demanded by thousands of parents and teachers who have long felt the need of such a book. There are plenty of little boys and girls who want to "speak a piece," and here is a book full of exactly what they require—short and easy dialogues, made up of short, easy parts, on subjects that their little minds can thoroughly understand, so that the speakers will find no difficulty in committing their respective parts to memory, even before they have learned to read. Paper covers. Price..................30 cts.
Bound in boards, cloth back..................50 cts.

Howard's Book of Drawing-Room Theatricals.
A collection of twelve short and amusing plays in one act and one scene, specially adapted for private performances; with practical directions for their preparation and management. Some of the plays are adapted for performers of one sex only. This book is just what is wanted by those who purpose getting up an entertainment of private theatricals: it contains all the necessary instructions for insuring complete success. 180 pages.

Paper cover. Price...30 cts.
Bound in boards with cloth back..................................50 cts.

Hudson's Private Theatricals for Home Performance.
A collection of Humorous Plays suitable for an Amateur Entertainment, with directions how to carry out a performance successfully. Some of the plays in this collection are adapted for performance by males only, others require only females for the cast, and all of them are in one scene and one act, and may be represented in any moderate sized parlor, without much preparation of costume or scenery. 180 pages.

Paper covers. Price...30 cts
Bound in boards with cloth back..................................50 cts

The Art of Dressing Well.
By Miss S. A. Frost. This book is designed for ladies and gentlemen who desire to make a favorable impression upon society, and is intended to meet the requirements of any season, place, or time; to offer such suggestions as will be valuable to those just entering society; to brides, for whose guidance a complete trousseau is described; to persons in mourning; indeed, to every individual who pays attention to the important objects of economy, style, and propriety of costume. 188 pages.

Paper covers. Price...30 cts
Bound in boards, cloth back.......................................50 cts

How to Amuse an Evening Party.
A complete collection of Home Recreations, including Round Games, Forfeits, Parlor Magic, Puzzles, and Comic Diversions; together with a great variety of Scientific Recreations and Evening Amusements. Profusely illustrated with nearly two hundred fine woodcuts. Here is family amusement for the million. Here is parlor or drawing-room entertainment, night after night, for a whole winter. A young man with this volume may render himself the *beau ideal* of a delightful companion at every party. He may take the lead in amusing the company, and win the hearts of all the ladies, and charm away the obduracy of the stoniest-hearted parent, by his powers of entertainment.

Bound in ornamental paper cover. Price............................30 cts.
Bound in boards, with cloth back..................................50 cts.

Martine's Droll Dialogues and Laughable Recitations.
By Arthur Martine, author of "Martine's Letter-Writer," etc., etc. A collection of Humorous Dialogues, Comic Recitations, Brilliant Burlesques, Spirited Stump Speeches, and Ludicrous Farces, adapted for School Celebrations and Home Amusement. 188 pages.

Paper covers. Price...30 cts.
Bound in boards, with cloth back..................................50 cts.

Frost's Humorous and Exhibition Dialogues
This is a collection of sprightly original Dialogues, in Prose and Verse, intended to be spoken at School Exhibitions. Some of the pieces are for boys, some for girls, while a number are designed to be used by both sexes. The Dialogues are all good, and will recommend themselves to those who desire to have innocent fun—the prevailing feature at a school celebration. 180 pages.

Paper cover. Price..30 cts
Bound in boards...50 cts

Popular Books sent Free of Postage at the Prices annexed.

Lester's "Look to the East."—(Webb Work.) A Ritual of the First Three Degrees of Masonry. Containing the complete work of the Entered Apprentice, Fellow Craft and Master Mason's Degrees, and their Ceremonies, Lectures, etc. Edited by Ralph P. Lester. This complete and beautiful Pocket Manual of the First Three Degrees of Masonry is printed in clear, legible type, and not obscured by any attempts at cypher or other perplexing contractions. It differs entirely from all other Manuals from the fact that it contains neither the passwords, grips, nor any other purely esoteric matter with which Masons, and Masons only, are necessarily entirely familiar. It affords, therefore, a thorough and valuable guide to the regular "work" in the above Degrees, divested of everything that any member of the Fraternity would object to see in print, or hesitate to carry in his pocket.

It embraces the correct routine of Opening and Closing the Lodge in each Degree; calling off and on; calling the Lodge up and down; the regular Order of Business; together with the entire Ceremonies of Initiating, Passing and Raising Candidates, as well as the Lectures of each Degree, all Ritually and Monitorally complete. Bound in cloth..............$2 00
Bound in Leather Tucks (pocket-book style), gilt edges...........$2 50

Dick's Recitations and Readings. No. 1. Comprising a carefully compiled selection of Humorous, Pathetic, Eloquent, Patriotic and Sentimental Pieces in Poetry and Prose; exclusively designed for Recitation or Reading. Edited by Wm. B. Dick. This is the first of a Series, uniform in size and style, which will include everything that is fresh and popular, introducing also some of the older gems of the English language that are always in demand, but excluding everything that is not eminently appropriate either for Declamation or Public Reading. Paper cover. **30 cts.**
16mo, full cloth..**50 cts.**

Frost's Proverbs and Charades. Containing a collection of Original Proverbs and Charades, some of which are for Dramatic Performance, and others arranged for Tableaux-Vivants. By S. A. Frost. This book comprises a selection of Acting Proverbs and ingenious Charades; a portion of them in the form of short and sprightly comedies, and the remainder arranged to be represented by Tableaux, all the details of which are clearly described. They are all taken from "The Parlor Stage" by the same author. 16mo, illuminated paper cover.............**30 cts.**
Bound in boards...**50 cts.**

Frost's Parlor Acting Charades. Intended solely for Performance in the Drawing-Room, and requiring no expensive Scenery or Properties to render them effective. By S. A. Frost. These excellent and original Charades are arranged as short parlor Comedies and Farces, full of brilliant repartee and amusing situations. They are selected from "The Parlor Stage" by the same author. 16mo, illuminated paper cover...**30 cts.**
16mo, illuminated boards..**50 cts.**

Burton's Amateur Actor. A Complete Guide to Private Theatricals; giving plain directions for arranging, decorating and lighting the Stage and its appurtenances; with rules and suggestions for mounting, rehearsing and performing all kinds of Plays, Parlor Pantomimes and Shadow Pantomimes. Illustrated with numerous engravings, and including a selection of original Plays, with Prologues, Epilogues, etc. By C. E. Burton. 16mo, illuminated paper cover...........................**30 cts.**
Bound in boards..**50 cts.**

Chips from Uncle Sam's Jack-knife. Illustrated with over 100 Comical Engravings, and comprising a collection of over 500 Laughable Stories, Funny Adventures, Comic Poetry. Large octavo. Price, **25 cts.**

Popular Books sent Free of Postage at the Prices annexed.

Day's Book-keeping Without a Master. Containing the Rudiments of Book-keeping in Single and Double Entry, together with the proper Forms and Rules for opening and keeping Condensed and General Book Accounts. This work is printed in a beautiful script type, and hence combines the advantages of a handsome style of writing with its very simple and easily understood lessons in Book-keeping. It presents a *fac-simile* of a handsomely written set of account books—on a small scale, it is true, but very neat and pretty. This will enable the learner to improve his hand-writing, while perfecting himself as an expert, or first-class accountant—which is done by frequent practice. The book exhibits all the different forms of Accounts, Balance Sheets, Trial-Balance, Commercial and Monetary Letters, Drafts, Notes, Credits, Orders, Inquiries, Replies, etc., etc., arranged in the script type exactly as they should be written for business purposes. This feature makes the work invaluable as a book of reference. The several pages have explanations at the bottom, to assist the learner, in small type. As a pattern for opening book-accounts it is especially valuable—particularly for those who are not well posted in the art. DAY'S BOOK-KEEPING is the size of a regular quarto Account Book, and is made to lie flat open, for convenience in use. Price.................50 Cts.

Blank Books for Day's Book-keeping. We have for sale Books of 96 pages each, ruled according to the patterns mentioned on page 3 of DAY'S BOOK-KEEPING, suitable for practice of the learner, viz.: No. 1—For General Book-keeping, pages 4 and 5; for Cash Account on page 13; for Day Book in Single Entry, pages 15 to 25. No 2—For Condensed Accounts, pages 9 and 10; for Cash Accounts, page 12; for Journal in Double Entry, pages 34 to 43. No. 3—For Ledgers in Double or Single Entry, pages 26 to 44. Price, each.................50 Cts.

How to Write a Composition. This original work will be found a valuable aid in writing a composition on any topic. It lays down plain directions for the division of a subject into its appropriate heads, and for arranging them in their natural order, commencing with the simplest theme and advancing progressively to the treatment of more complicated subjects. The use of this excellent hand-book will save the student the many hours of labor too often wasted in trying to write a plain composition. It affords a perfect skeleton of each subject, with its headings or divisions clearly defined, and each heading filled in with the ideas which the subject suggests; so that all the writer has to do, in order to produce a good composition, is to enlarge on them to suit his taste and inclination. Bound in boards, cloth back. Price.................50 Cts.

Nugent's Burlesque and Musical Acting Charades. Containing ten Charades, all in different styles, two of which are easy and effective Comic Parlor Operas, with Music and Pianoforte Accompaniments. These Plays require no scenery, and the dialogue is short, witty, and easy to learn. To each Charade will be found an introductory note, containing hints for its performance. Paper cover. Price.................30 Cts.
Bound in boards, cloth back.................50 Cts.

Snipsnaps and Snickerings of Simon Snodgrass. These funny and amusing stories are illustrative of Irish Drolleries, Ludicrous Dutch Blunders, Yankee Tricks and Dodges, Backwoods Boasting, Negro Comicalities, Perilous Pranks of Fighting Men, Frenchmen's Queer Mistakes, and other phases of eccentric character to make a complete Medley of Wit and Humor. Full of funny engravings. Price.................25 cts.

The Strange and Wonderful Adventures of Bachelor Butterfly. Showing his Hairbreadth Escapes from fire and cold—his being come over by a Widow with nine small children—and his firm endurance of these and other perils of a most extraordinary nature. The whole illustrated by about 200 engravings. Price.................30 cts.

Popular Books sent Free of Postage at the Prices annexed.

Martine's Letter-writer and Etiquette Combined. For the use of Ladies and Gentlemen. 12mo., cloth, gilt side and back. A great many books have been printed on the subject of etiquette and correct behavior in society, but none of them are sufficiently comprehensive and matter-of-fact enough to suit the class of people who may be called new beginners in fashionable life. This book is entirely different from others in that respect. It explains in a plain, common-sense way, precisely how to conduct yourself in every position in society. This book also contains over 300 sensible letters and notes suitable to every occasion in life, and is probably the best treatise on Letter-writing that has ever been printed. It gives easily understood directions that are brief and to the point. It has some excellent model letters of friendship and business, and its model Love Letters are unequaled. If any lady or gentleman desires to know how to *begin* a love correspondence, this is just the book they want. This volume contains the same matter as "Martine's Hand-book of Etiquette," and "Martine's Sensible Letter-writer," and, in fact, combines those two books bound together in one substantial volume of 373 pages........**$1 50**

Row's National Wages Tables. Showing at a glance the amount of wages, from half an hour to sixty hours, at from $1 to $37 per week. Also from one-quarter of a day to four weeks, at $1 to $37 per per week. By Nelson Row. By this book, which is particularly useful when part of a week, day, or hour is lost, a large pay-roll can be made out in a few minutes, thus saving more time in making out one pay-roll than the cost of the book. Every employer hiring help by the hour, day or week, should get a copy; and every employee should also obtain one, as it will enable him to know exactly the amount of money he is entitled to on pay-day. 12mo, 80 pages. Half bound........**50 cts.**
Cloth ....**75 cts.**
Roan Tuck **$1.00**

The Young Reporter; or, How to Write Short-Hand. A complete Phonographic Teacher, intended to afford thorough instruction to those who have not the assistance of an Oral Teacher. By the aid of this work, any person of the most ordinary intelligence may learn to write Short-Hand, and report Speeches and Sermons in a short time. Bound in boards, with cloth back........**50 cts.**

The Yankee Cook Book. *A New System of Cookery.* Containing hundreds of excellent receipts from actual experience in Cooking; also, full explanations in the art of Carving. 126 pages. Illuminated paper cover........**30 cts.**
Bound in boards, cloth back........**50 cts.**

Mother Shipton's Oriental Dream Book. Being a reliable Interpretation of Dreams, Visions, Apparitions, etc. Together with a history of remarkable Dreams, proven true as interpreted. Collected and arranged from the most celebrated Masters. 16mo, 118 pages. Illuminated paper cover........**30 cts.**

Jack Johnson's Jokes for the Jolly. A collection of Astonishing Anecdotes, Weird Witticisms, Side-Splitting Stories, and Mirthful Morsels for the Melancholy. Providing a sure solace for sadness, a balm for the blues, and an active antidote against all aches. 128 pages, 16mo. Illuminated paper cover........**25 cts.**

Day's Conversation Cards. *A New Original Set. Comprising Eighteen Questions and Twenty-four Answers, so arranged that the whole of the Answers are Apt Replies to each one of the Eighteen Questions.* The Set comprises forty-two Cards in the aggregate, which are put up in a handsome case, with printed directions for use........**30 cts.**

Popular Books sent Free of Postage at the Prices annexed

The American Home Cook Book.
Containing several hundred excellent Recipes. The whole based on many years' experience of an American Housewife. Illustrated with Engravings. All the Recipes in this book are written from actual experiments in Cooking. There are no copyings from theoretical cooking recipes.
Bound in boards, cloth back. Price..50 cts.
Bound in paper covers. Price...30 cts.

Amateur Theatricals and Fairy-Tale Dramas.
A collection of original plays, expressly designed for Drawing-room performance. By S. A. Frost. This work is designed to meet a want, which has been long felt, of short and amusing pieces suitable to the limited stage of the private parlor. The old friends of fairy-land will be recognized among the Fairy-Tale Dramas, newly clothed and arranged.
Paper covers. Price..30 cts.
Bound in boards, with cloth back...50 cts.

Parlor Tricks with Cards.
Containing explanations of Tricks and Deceptions with Playing Cards, embracing Tricks with Cards performed by Sleight-of-hand, by the aid of Memory, Mental Calculation and Arrangement of the Cards, by the aid of Confederacy; and Tricks performed by the aid of Prepared Cards. The whole illustrated and made plain and easy, with 70 engravings. This book is an abridgment of our large work, entitled "The Secret Out."
Paper covers. Price...30 cts.
Bound in boards, with cloth back..50 cts.

Chesterfield's Letter-writer and Complete Book of Etiquette;
or, Concise, Systematic Directions for Arranging and Writing Letters. Also, Model Correspondence in Friendship and Business, and a great variety of Model Love Letters. This work is also a Complete Book of Etiquette. There is more real information in this book than in half a dozen volumes of the most expensive ones.
Bound in boards, with cloth back. Price..35 cts.

Frank Converse's Complete Banjo Instructor.
Without a Master. Containing a choice collection of Banjo Solos, Hornpipes, Reels, Jigs, Walk Arounds, Songs, and Banjo Stories, progressively arranged and plainly explained. Bound in boards, with cloth back. Price.......50 cts.

The Magician's Own Book.
Containing several hundred amusing Sleight-of-hand and Card Tricks, Perplexing Puzzles, Entertaining Tricks and Secret Writing Explained. Illustrated with over 500 wood engravings. 12mo., cloth, gilt side and back stamp. Price..........$1 50

North's Book of Love Letters.
With Directions how to write and when to use them, and 120 specimen Letters, suitable for Lovers of any age and condition, and under all circumstances. Interspersed with the author's comments thereon. The whole forming a convenient handbook of valuable information and counsel for the use of those who need friendly guidance and advice in matters of Love, Courtship and Marriage. By Ingoldsby North. This book is recommended to all who are from any cause in doubt as to the manner in which they should write or reply to letters upon love and courtship. The reader will be aided in his thoughts—he will see where he is likely to please and where to displease, how to begin and how to end his letter, and how to judge of those nice shades of expression and feeling concerning which a few mistaken expressions may create misunderstanding. All who wish not only to copy a love letter, but to learn the art of writing them, will find North's book a very pleasant, sensible and friendly companion. It is an additional recommendation that the variety offered is very large. Cloth. Price..75 cts.
Bound in boards..50 cts.

Popular Books sent Free of Postage at the Prices annexed.

What Shall We Do To-Night? *or, Social Amusements for Evening Parties.* This Elegant Book affords an almost inexhaustible fund of Amusement for Evening Parties, Social Gatherings, and all Festive Occasions, ingeniously grouped together so as to furnish complete and ever-varying entertainment for *Twenty-six Evenings.* Its repertoire embraces all the best Round and Forfeit Games, clearly described and rendered perfectly plain by original and amusing examples; interspersed with a great variety of Ingenious Puzzles, Entertaining Tricks, and Innocent Sells; new and original *Musical* and *Poetical Pastimes,* Startling Illusions, and Mirth-provoking Exhibitions; including complete directions and text for performing *Charades, Tableaux, Parlor Pantomimes,* the world-renowned *Punch and Judy, Gallanty Shows,* and original *Shadow Pantomimes*; also, full information for the successful performance of *Dramatic Dialogues* and *Parlor Theatricals,* with a selection of Original Plays, etc., written expressly for this work. It is embellished with over one hundred descriptive and explanatory engravings, and contains 366 pages, printed on fine toned paper. 12mo, bound in extra cloth.................$2.00

How To Conduct a Debate. A Series of Complete Debates, Outlines of Debates, and Questions for Discussion; with references to the best sources of information on each particular topic. In the Complete Debates, the questions for discussion are defined, the debate formally opened, an array of brilliant arguments adduced on either side, and the debate closed according to Parliamentary usages. The second part consists of Questions for Debate, with heads of arguments, for and against, given in a condensed form for the speakers to enlarge upon to suit their own fancy. In addition to these are a large collection of good Debatable Questions. The authorities, to be referred to for information, being given at the close of every debate throughout the work. By Frederic Rowton. 232 pages, 16mo, paper cover......................................50 cts.
Bound in boards, cloth back...75 cts.

McBride's Comic Dialogues *for School Exhibitions and Literary Entertainments.* A collection of original Humorous Dialogues, especially designed for the development and display of Amateur Dramatic Talent, and introducing a variety of sentimental, sprightly, comic, and genuine Yankee characters. By H. Elliott McBride. 16mo, illuminated paper cover..30 cts.
Bound in boards..50 cts.

The Fireside Magician; *or, The Art of Natural Magic made Easy*—being a familiar and scientific explanation of Legerdemain, Physical Amusement, Recreative Chemistry, Diversions with Cards, and of all the minor mysteries of Mechanical Magic, with feats as performed in public by Herr Alexander and Robert Houdin. 132 pages, 16mo, illuminated paper cover..30 cts.
Bound in boards, cloth back..50 cts.

Frost's Original Letter-Writer, *and Laws and By-Laws of American Society Combined.* Being a complete collection of original Letters and Notes upon every imaginable subject of every-day life, and a condensed but thorough treatise on Etiquette, and its usages in America. This work includes a dictionary of synonyms especially adapted for the use of correspondents. By S. A. Frost. 16mo, 378 pages, extra cloth, gilt..$1.50

Row's Complete Fractional Ready Reckoner. For buying and selling any kind of merchandise, giving the fractional parts of a pound, yard, etc., from one quarter to one thousand, at any price from one-quarter of a cent to five dollars. By Nelson Row. 16mo, 253 pages. Boards..50 cts

Popular Books sent Free of Postage at the Prices annexed.

Book of Household Pets.
Containing valuable instructions about the Diseases, Breeding, Training and Management of the Canary, Mocking Bird, Brown Thrush, or Thrasher, and other birds, and the rearing and management of all kinds of Pigeons and Fancy Poultry, Rabbits, Squirrels, Guinea Pigs, White Mice and Dogs; together with a Comprehensive Treatise on the Principle and Management of the Salt and Fresh Water Aquarium. Illustrated with 125 fine wood-cuts. In boards. Price.50 cts. Bound in cloth, gilt side..75 cts.

Athletic Sports for Boys.
A Repository of Graceful Recreations for Youth, containing clear and complete instructions in Gymnastics, Limb Exercises, Jumping, Pole Leaping, Dumb Bells, Indian Clubs, Parallel Bars, the Horizontal Bar, the Trapeze, the Suspended Ropes, Skating, Swimming, Rowing, Sailing, Horsemanship, Riding, Driving, Angling, Fencing and Broadsword. The whole splendidly illustrated with 194 fine wood-cuts and diagrams. Bound in boards, with cloth back. Price.75 cts. Bound in cloth, gilt side..$1 00

The Bar-Tender's Guide; or, How to Mix all Kinds of
Fancy Drinks. Containing clear and reliable directions for mixing all the beverages used in the United States. Embracing Punches, Juleps, Cobblers, Cocktails, etc., etc., in endless variety. By Jerry Thomas. With plain directions for making Syrups, Bitters, Cordials and Liqueurs, with the various harmless flavoring and coloring substances used in their preparation, and complete instructions for Distilling, Filtering and Clarifying them.
Illuminated paper cover...50 cts. Bound in full cloth..75 cts.

How to Learn the Sense of 3,000 French Words in One
Hour. This ingenious little book actually accomplishes all that its title claims. It is a fact that there are at least three thousand words in the French language, forming a large proportion of those used in ordinary conversation, which are spelled exactly the same as in English, or become the same by very slight and easily understood changes in their termination.
16mo, illuminated paper cover...................................25 cts. Bound in full cloth..50 cts.

Barton's Comic Recitations and Humorous Dialogues.
Containing a variety of Comic Recitations in Prose and Poetry, Amusing Dialogues, Burlesque Scenes, Eccentric Orations and Stump Speeches, Humorous Interludes and Laughable Farces. Designed for School Commencements and Amateur Theatricals. Edited by Jerome Barton. This is the best collection of Humorous pieces, especially adapted to the parlor stage, that has ever been published. Illuminated paper cover. Price.....30 cts. Bound in boards, with cloth back.................................50 cts.

The Secret Out; or, One Thousand Tricks with Cards, and
other Recreations. Illustrated with over Three Hundred Engravings. A book which explains all the Tricks and Deceptions with Playing Cards ever known, and gives, besides, a great many new ones—the whole being described so carefully, with engravings to illustrate them, that anybody can easily learn how to perform them. This work also contains 240 of the best Tricks in Legerdemain, in addition to the card tricks. 12mo, 400 pages, bound in cloth, with gilt side and back. Price......................$1 50

Lander's Expose of Odd-Fellowship.
Containing all the Lectures complete, with regulations for Opening, Conducting and Closing a Lodge; together with Forms of Initiation, Charges of the various Offices, etc., giving all the Works in the following Degrees: 1st or White Degree: 2d or Covenant Degree; 3d or Royal Blue Degree; 4th or Remembrance Degree; 5th or Scarlet Degree. Paper cover............................25 cts.

www.ingramcontent.com/pod-product-compliance
Lightning Source LLC
Chambersburg PA
CBHW030341170426
43202CB00010B/1198